The Ultimate Guide to Evaluating Mr. Right and Eliminating Mr. Wrong

Corey Guyton, Ph.D.

Durham, North Carolina

http://www.thegenuinescholar.com

www.facebook.com/mrright.mrwrong

Acknowledgements

A special thanks to everyone who gave me feedback on this manuscript. This includes family, friends, and colleagues. I would like to specifically thank Aleasha Motley, Latesha Rutledge, and Justina Lindsey for their careful attention and suggestions.

Cover Design by Ilian G.

Edited by Allison H.

Contents

Preface

I have received email after email, phone call after phone call, and visit after visit from women who are tired of meeting guys who are misleading, toxic, selfish, and manipulating. The story is usually the same: women have invested many hours into these men, and they are left with nothing to show for their invested time. The result is typically frustrated women who have a lowered self-esteem and a decline in their trust for men. Hearing these types of stories every day has pained my heart and created a desire for me to help. This book is one avenue I have taken to help women avoid ending up in these types of unhealthy situations.

The content in this book is derived from the common relationship issues I have heard while coaching and counseling women. There are three key areas that I have learned that a lot of women struggle with, which I address in this book:

1. Self-Esteem and Self-Value
2. Understanding the Concept of Healthy Dating
3. Ways to Effectively Evaluate a Good Man

The reality is that a lot of women get attention from guys, but it is hard for them to determine which guys are looking for a genuine relationship and which guys are about games. By reading this book, women should be able to identify which guys are in it for the long haul and which guys are trying to take advantage of them. Readers should also gain a sense of confidence from having a better understanding of their self-worth and value, while also understanding the true meaning of dating.

I want readers to know that this book did not happen overnight and has been in the making for years. I could not fully write it until I put in the necessary hours coaching and counseling, so that I could address the most pertinent issues women were facing while dating. I wrote a book a few years ago, titled "*Through the Eyes of a Man: The Truth about College Dating Revealed to Women*," and worked the college circuit for a few years. Although I enjoyed working with college students and helping them with their dating challenges, I found that older women would constantly ask me about a resource for them. After years of promising that I would create a resource for them, I have finally created a page-turning book that is sure to help them with dating.

Becoming a Relationship Expert

My journey dates back to my high school days. I was a very respectable young man and treated women with the utmost respect. Throughout my high school years, I remained a virgin and did not receive a lot of attention from the ladies. Most girls thought I was a nice guy and a great friend, but they did not see me as boyfriend material. To make matters worse, I was a little chubby and I attributed the lack of attention to my weight. I graduated high school without ever having a real girlfriend. I told myself that once I went to college, I was going to lose weight and make all the girls who did not give me any attention in high school wish they had considered me.

As I promised myself, I lost 30 pounds during my first year as an undergraduate. The change in weight resulted in more attention from the ladies, and I gained more confidence. I went from being many girls' "friend" to the guy they wanted to date.

Toward the end of my freshman year of college, I got involved with Student Orientation. Student Orientation was a program that brought freshmen in before the start of school to help with their transition from high school to college. Being a part of Orientation gave me the opportunity to meet incoming freshmen prior to the start of school and also to "mark my territory" before anyone else. I knew that freshmen females were excited about coming to college and were intrigued by older men, so this worked out to my advantage.

In addition to Orientation, my friends and I ("The Crew") hosted the first party of the year at our apartment. We always invited freshmen to our parties and we knew they would come because I was "that guy from Orientation." This always resulted in us having the biggest parties with the most women. To make sure there was no competition, we limited the number of guys who came.

A combination of The Crew hosting some of the best parties on campus, the exposure I received at Orientation, and joining a fraternity early in my sophomore year resulted in me becoming fairly popular on campus. Overnight, I literally went from being a guy who did not get much attention to getting an overflow of it. I thoroughly enjoyed the new attention because it made up for the attention I did not receive in high school.

This newfound attention and status created opportunities for me to date multiple women. I quickly realized that I could get almost anything I wanted from women without being in a committed relationship. I felt that if I got into a relationship, it would take away from the attention I was receiving, and that was not a sacrifice I was willing to make. I went through my entire undergraduate career without ever being in a committed relationship.

During my undergraduate career, I misled a few women. Although I never stated that we would be in a committed relationship, I always showcased actions that made them think that we were. For example, I used terms of endearment such as "baby," "honey," and "sweetheart" to make them feel as if they were my girlfriends. I made sure that I chose my words carefully and stated them in a way that never officially declared that I wanted anything other than a friendship. I would say things like, "Right now is not the time for me to be in a relationship, but who knows what could happen." Ultimately, my goal was to make sure that once I parted ways with a woman, she would never be able to say I did her wrong.

This behavior lasted until I got to graduate school. At this point, I realized that I wanted a serious relationship. During my second year of graduate school, I opened myself up to a relationship and fell in love for the first time. I promised myself that whenever I decided to really settle down, I would be the best boyfriend ever and completely faithful to my significant other. I stayed true to this promise and was a really good boyfriend.

Then out of nowhere, my girlfriend at the time approached me and stated that God had placed it on her heart to end our relationship. I did not understand this at the time and was really broken, because I knew I was the perfect boyfriend and had made every effort to treat her like a queen. I did not want to believe that God would allow her to walk away from me, especially when I felt I was doing everything right. Completely heartbroken, I flew home to Georgia. Luckily, I had the support of my best friend, who allowed me to sleep on his couch while I coped with the breakup.

In hindsight, I knew the breakup was mandated by God and now I can say that I really appreciate her for following His guidance. Although she had no true explanation about why we needed to break up, she knew that she had to be obedient. Over the years, I realized the breakup was one of the best things that could have ever happened to me, because it is a big part of the reason I became a relationship expert.

At the moment my ex-girlfriend broke up with me, I realized that the pain I was feeling was the same pain I inflicted on others during my time in undergrad. My thinking about leading women on and being careless with their hearts changed drastically, because prior to being hurt myself, I did not understand why women took breakups so hard. I used to have the mindset that they would eventually get over it. I promised myself that from that moment on, I would never again inflict that type of pain on anyone else.

I made a vow to be celibate for two years, and I was successful in upholding this promise. During this time, I had an opportunity to get my life back on track with God and I discovered part of my purpose in life: to empower others to discover their value and to strive for the best in every aspect of their lives. As a result, I began to mentor young ladies by helping them avoid getting into situations that would cause high levels of pain and I started mentoring young men on what it means to be a man and how our misconceptions of manhood cause us to treat women badly. I also took the initiative to start helping women who were in unhealthy relationships by giving them advice and empowerment to help overcome their situations. One of the biggest rewards I received for being obedient to God and for taking a vow of celibacy is the beautiful queen I found, whom I eventually married.

I really feel that God allowed me to experience life so I could eventually come back and help others avoid making the same mistakes. I believe every action has consequences and God took me through a period of restoration – my two years away from dating. Now, six years later, I am now restored and blessed.

The truth is that deep down inside I was always a guy who had high values. My true identity was the respectful guy in high school who did not get a lot of attention. I created an identity in college that was phony, because I wanted to try and make up for all of the attention I felt I did not receive. I also had a skewed perception of what it meant to be a man. As a member of a fraternity and a guy who was seen as popular on campus, I felt that my manhood was linked to the number of women I could have on my team.

The Relationship Expert

My role as a college administrator played a major role in my becoming a relationship expert. One of the biggest moments in my administrative career that pushed me to want to help young women even more was when I sat on a panel with undergraduate men about dating in college. A young lady in the audience asked the question, "How do men view women whom they've slept with on the first night?" One undergraduate panel participant stated that it did not change the way he viewed those women. I was appalled by the answer because I felt it was a lie, but I gave him the benefit of the doubt. The young man seated next to me leaned over and asked me to answer the question, because he said that if he answered the question truthfully, it would destroy his "game." This made me realize that college-aged men do not like to truthfully discuss these topics, because they are currently "playing the game" of manipulating women and sleeping around, and revealing the truth would hurt their ability to play it.

After coming to this realization, I quickly started doing relationship presentations on campus for young ladies to attend. The presentations became very popular, and I quickly found my office flooded with young women asking me for relationship advice. Also at the time, I started getting offers from other schools to present about college dating, because they had heard about my presentations. I started accepting these offers and I was eventually asked by a lot of young women to write a book about college dating. As a result, I wrote my first book, *Through the Eyes of a Man: The Truth about College Dating Revealed to Women*.

After publishing my first book, I started giving relationship advice on YouTube, Facebook, and my blog. The response from my advice was amazing, and I started receiving tons of emails from people who had viewed my works asking for advice. I started giving advice, and, as they say, the rest is history…

CHAPTER 1

INTRODUCTION

In today's society, where do you learn the proper ways to date? Is it from your parents? Social media? Television? Or do you just figure it out on your own? One of the biggest problems is that people do not know where to go to learn how to properly date, especially if they do not have good examples of dating in their homes or in their communities. Some people come from environments where their parents have been in continuous unhealthy relationships, and their perception of dating is based on what they have seen in their homes; others watch television shows and learn their dating habits from "reality stars"; and, more recently, a lot of people are depending on their friends to post statuses on social media sites about relationships to gain an understanding of dating.

Over the last five years, I have been blessed to serve as a relationship expert and have given advice to tons of individuals. I love my job, but it constantly reminds me that dating is not easy and can be very complex. It saddens my heart to hear story after story of young ladies who give their heart to a man with the hopes of forming a healthy relationship, but end up being used, abused, and misled.

The results of these situations are usually women who are very upset and angry at men, and the trauma experienced from the hurt causes them to put walls up around their hearts. In extreme circumstances, some women get to a point where they become cold and literally hate all men. This is when these women start getting labeled as "bitter" by a lot of men and are made to feel that they are wrong for having the feelings they have.

I am a strong ally for these women, because I know that their negative emotions did not happen by osmosis and are more than likely a result of a traumatic relationship with a man. After many consultations, I came to the realization that a lot of women did not know how to properly date and were being manipulated by men who took advantage of this lack of knowledge. For these reasons, I wrote this book to help women learn how to properly date, while also learning ways to effectively evaluate a man, with the hopes that they will lower their chances of getting into another unhealthy relationship.

Before I go any further and give you tips about evaluating men, I want to debunk a huge myth that has caused a lot of women to lose hope in dating.

Myth: There are no more good men left to date.

There are a lot of good men out there, but sometimes they are not as visible as the men who are no good. The reality is that good men are not as exciting to talk about and do not make for good conversation. We constantly hear about guys who cheat, manipulate, and hurt women, but we rarely hear about guys who love and respect women. In addition, the media will not report stories about men who treat women with respect, the Internet hardly ever promotes stories about men who treat women with respect, and most guys who treat women with respect are not in the limelight and are typically focused on being productive in life.

There is a lot of danger to this myth, because it causes some women to give up on love because they see no reason to try if there are not any good men available. This is also dangerous because some women feel they have to settle for a man of lesser quality because the pool of good men is too small and they feel their odds of getting one is slim to none. The truth is that good men are out there, but it may take a little patience and you must learn how to identify them. Hopefully I will be able to help you with this book. My advice is based on the countless successful and unsuccessful stories I have studied, heard, and experienced. As you read the book, I encourage you to:

- Have an open heart
- Take time to reflect on what you read
- Ask yourself how you can apply some of the knowledge to your life

I wish you happy readings, and I pray that you are able to achieve the relationship you desire to have.

The Mis-education of Dating

In the 21st century, the definition of the word *dating* has become so vague that no one really knows the true meaning. This is a huge part of the reason why so many people have issues when they are trying to establish a relationship, because both individuals are on two different communication lines and they each have their personal definition for dating. For one person, dating could simply mean hanging out, without any intentions of progressing towards anything more, while the other person feels they are on the path towards marriage. This creates a conflict of interest and has the potential to be a recipe for disaster. I believe that healthy dating starts with having a healthy understanding of what dating means.

As a relationship expert, I have attended hundreds of panels and discussions about dating. The one constant at all of these events is that almost everyone disagrees on the definition of healthy dating. This book is a reflection of what I feel healthy dating is, based on my experiences and expertise.

What is Dating?

Dating is the process of two individuals engaging in social activities for the purpose of evaluating each other's suitability as a potential intimate partner. In this definition, there are a few key terms that you need to focus on that will help you achieve healthy dating. These words are *process*, *social activities*, *purpose*, and *evaluating*.

Process

It is very important to understand that dating is a *process*, meaning that it consists of steps and is not meant to be quick. One of the biggest mistakes I see is that a lot of people tend to take a "microwave" approach to dating instead of a "crock-pot" approach. People want quick results and instant satisfaction, so they date in overdrive and commit to a person without really getting to know them. Throughout this book, you will realize that I am big on taking a slow, crock-pot approach. When food is cooked in a microwave, the quality of it is less than stellar, and there is a lot left to be desired. On the contrary, when food is cooked in a crock-pot, the slow process tends to create a quality product.

Social Activities

Social is the key word. I have countless discussions with individuals who meet someone and quickly move beyond social activities into more intimate activities. While dating, it is very important to keep your interactions more social than intimate – hence, the words *social activities*. Social activities allow you time to get to know a person mentally, spiritually, and emotionally.

One of the biggest misunderstandings people have is that they think social activities pertaining to dating mean spending money. Healthy dating is not about spending a lot of money; instead, it is about getting to know the other person. This means that you do not necessarily have to go to an expensive restaurant, movie, or any other activity that requires a lot of money; instead, you can visit a park, walk on a nature trail, go to happy hour at a bar, or eat frozen yogurt.

Purpose

Healthy dating is meaningful dating and has purpose. The term *dating* insinuates that there is purpose to a social outing with a person, and that purpose is usually to discover if that person has the potential to be your mate. If these are not the intentions, then I would argue that you are technically not dating;

instead, I would say that you are going out on a social outing without any intentions.

Evaluating

Although dating can be fun and exciting, there is a serious side that must be present in order to be healthy. This serious side is the evaluation process. The truth is that healthy relationships are formed when proper evaluation occurs. The purpose for dating is to see if a person is compatible with you, so you must always assess the person you are dating to determine if they are the one for you.

Why Evaluation Over Finding?

Before you get too far in this book, I would like to make it clear that I am somewhat of a traditionalist. I have an old-school spiritual approach to dating, hence the reason the title includes the word "evaluating" instead of "finding." My philosophy is that a man should find a woman, and this philosophy is based on my personal experience as a relationship expert and my Christian upbringing, which states that "whoso findeth a wife findeth a good thing." In today's society, it seems that this Bible verse has been reversed to "whoso findeth a husband findeth a good thing." This reversal of roles is the result of a lot of women believing that there are not many good men left, causing them to take the role of the pursuer and not the pursued.

When I have relationship seminars and I give my philosophy on dating, a lot of people look at me as if I am a three-headed monster. They typically tell me that my approach is out-of-date in the 21st century. They usually feel that women should be able to pursue and select a man. I can admit that, in some cases, when a woman pursues a man, they end up in a healthy relationship; but far too often, I have seen the exact opposite happen, and the woman is left hurt. The one misconception about my philosophy on dating is that people feel I take away the selection process for a woman and give all of the power to the man. This is where the word "evaluating" comes into play.

When you evaluate a person, you have the power to determine if you would like to be with a person or not. Think of it as you being a queen on the throne. Queens do not look for or chase anyone; instead, others present themselves in front of the queen, and she determines if they are acceptable or not.

The truth is that when women begin aggressively pursuing men, it puts them at a disadvantage. If a woman chases a man, he has the ability to control the situation, because her pursuit lets him know that she likes him, which gives him the opportunity to make her work for him. In these situations, men do not have to take the time to get to know a woman internally, because there is no incentive to do so. At this point, men can push the envelope and try to be physical with a woman, because if it does not work out, he will not have lost anything because he was not pursuing her in the first place.

Secondly, there are a lot of guys who have learned the art of "appearing to be the perfect guy." If a woman does not learn how to effectively evaluate a man, she may be fooled by him and end up in an unhealthy situation. The truth is that finding someone is not hard to accomplish, but evaluating them is the true task. For all of these reasons, I suggest evaluating over finding a man.

I will end this chapter by giving you five things to think about pertaining to being pursued instead of pursuing.

- **When You are the Pursuer, You Go Where the Person You are Chasing Wants You to Go!**

This means that a man can lead you to the destination of his choice – friend with benefits, titleless relationship, or another situation other than what you desired. This causes you to waste time and extra energy trying to get him to reroute towards your ideal destination.

- **When You are Pursued, You Control the Destination**

This means that you control where the relationship goes, and if he does not follow you to your ideal destination (a relationship), then you will know he was not meant to arrive there with you.

- **People Tend to Value What they Work For**

If you want a guy to fully value and commit to you, make sure that he feels like he put in work to get you. I do not want you to misunderstand – a guy will accept what is given to him, but that does not mean he will value it.

- **Showing that You are Interested is Not the Same as Chasing**

You can let a man know that you are interested, but after he has this information, he should take over and begin the pursuit. The problem is that a lot of women state their interest and then aggressively start pursing the guy. This allows the guy to make the woman work for him, and more than likely, he can make her do whatever he wants her to do, because he knows she likes him.

- **His Pursuit is a Sign that He is Interested in You**

There is no foolproof way of assuring that a guy is working towards a relationship with you, but there are things you can do to try to lower the odds of being used. Having him work for you (initiating phone calls, taking you out, and proving he wants a committed relationship) will give you a better sense of peace and increase the odds of ending up in a committed relationship.

CHAPTER 2

HEALTHY DATING STARTS
WITH A HEALTHY YOU

At this point, you should have a solid understanding of the meaning of dating and the importance of learning how to evaluate a potential mate. Before we discuss strategies and tips for dating, I want to address an important element that often goes undiscussed. I meet tons of individuals who are looking for that special someone who will sweep them off their feet and carry them into the valley of love. Although this sounds great in theory, the reality is that some people are not prepared for this type of love, because they have areas in their lives that need to be addressed before they open their hearts to someone else.

A wise man once told me that a healthy relationship is not about two perfect individuals coming together; instead, it is about two whole people coming together. This means that you do not have to be perfect, but you must fill any voids you have before starting a relationship. If these voids are not filled, then the chances of a person being successful at dating decrease tremendously. Some people feel that they need another person to complete them, and this is a major mistake. The only time you should ever need another person to complete you is during an organ transplant, not a relationship. This chapter will address some of the common voids that hinder some women from successfully dating and finding real love. These voids are heartbreak, loneliness, and low self-esteem. I encourage you to evaluate yourself and see if you are whole and ready to step into the world of dating.

Heartbreak

It does not matter if you are masculine, feminine, nerdy, thuggish, laid back, prissy, preppy, rich, poor, gay, straight, male, or female, experiencing heartbreak is one of the most difficult things one could ever encounter. When I come across someone who is experiencing a fresh dose of heartbreak, I immediately say, "I understand." As strong as I claim to be, I can admit that heartbreak is one of the worst feelings I have ever experienced.

Some people see dating as the medicine to cure heartbreak. Unfortunately, this is not the answer. Introducing a new person into your life while you are still experiencing the symptoms of heartbreak is a recipe for disaster. The new person is only addressing the symptoms of your heartbreak (loneliness, low self-esteem, etc.) and not the root of your feelings. To put this into perspective, let's discuss a person who takes aspirin (new person) for their continuous headaches (heartbreak).

If someone has headache after headache, they may take aspirin to relieve the pain. The aspirin is designed to address the symptom of headaches, which is the pain, but it is not designed to cure the cause of the headaches. This is why the headaches are recurring, because there is an underlying issue that is causing the headaches, and the aspirin is only a temporary fix. If this person consulted with a trained medical professional, they may be able to get to the root of the problem, and the headaches will fade away, causing them to no longer need the aspirin.

I give this example because some of you are trying to medicate your pain from heartbreak with a new guy, but the reality is that you have to address the true problem and properly heal yourself of heartbreak so that the pain will naturally go away. I will give you a few steps to help you heal from heartbreak, so you will not have to depend on dating to mask the pain.

I.   **Allow Yourself Time to Grieve**

The first thing you must understand when dealing with heartbreak is that you are grieving the loss of a person. Typically, we associate *grieving* with death, but the definition of grief is "experiencing the pain of a loss." You are experiencing grief during heartbreak because you lost a person who was near and dear to your heart. I suggest that you take time for yourself and remember that recovery is a process and does not happen overnight.

II. **Accept that the Relationship is Over**

When you love someone and you put your time, energy, emotions, and heart into them, you do not want to see that person leave, and it is hard for you to accept that they are gone. Your mind can sometimes play tricks on you and make you believe that they will have an epiphany and realize they made a mistake by leaving you. The thought of the person possibly returning is one of the reasons it takes some people a long time to recover from a breakup. When you fully accept that a relationship is over, you can begin to heal and move forward.

III. Don't Blame or Compare Yourself to Another Person

When someone leaves you, you can find yourself asking the question, "What is wrong with me?" In many cases, there is nothing wrong with you. The real problem lies within your ex and the internal conflicts he is having. If you start blaming yourself for the reasons a person left, you will live a life of regrets, and it will hinder your ability to heal and recover.

Another thing I like to stress is that if your ex left you for another person, try not to compare yourself to that person or ask what makes the other person better than you. People leave relationships for different reasons, and they choose other people for various reasons. I can assure you that your value does not decline as a result of them leaving you. If you know you are valuable, you will see their departure as their loss. As the old cliché goes, one person's trash is another person's treasure, and you will be someone else's treasure if you allow yourself to properly heal.

IV. You Will Heal Only if You Want to Heal

The key to properly healing is to work towards improvement and not dig yourself further into depression. I fully understand that, early in the process of heartbreak, you may experience immense pain, and this is completely normal. The truth is that the only way you will heal is if you really want to heal. Sometimes people find comfort living in their self-pity, because it allows them to remain upset while also keeping them mentally and emotionally attached to their ex. When you get to the point where you move beyond the anger directed towards the other person and focus more on yourself, you will begin the real process of healing.

V.   Accept that You May Never Get Your Questions Answered

When someone breaks your heart, it is only normal for you to ask the question, "Why?" Unfortunately, you may never get your questions answered and, even if you do, you may never get an answer that you find acceptable. I have seen so many people stay mentally bound to a person because they desire answers. To fully recover from heartbreak, you have to come to a point where you fully accept the fact that you may never get an answer to your questions. The only person you need to question while dealing with heartbreak is yourself. You need to ask yourself, "Do I deserve better than getting my heart broken by this person and do I deserve to recover from this heartbreak to become happy again?"

VI.   The Further Away You Stay, the Easier It Will Be to Heal

The further away you can stay from a person after a breakup, the easier it is to recover. Think of it this way: a drug addict cannot properly recover from drug addiction if they are always around drugs; a person who is heartbroken cannot fully heal from heartbreak if they are around the person who caused the heartbreak.

If you find yourself dealing with any of these six steps above, then you are not ready to date or evaluate a man. I highly encourage you to focus on rebuilding yourself and stabilizing your emotions. Once you have successfully recovered from heartbreak, you will be at a point where you are ready to date in a healthy way.

Loneliness

In today's society, being single is sometimes seen as taboo. For some reason, people hate being single, and some feel they are being punished when they do not have a companion. As a result, people's fear of being single causes them to date uncontrollably and settle for less than love. This opens up the door for these individuals to date people whom they would normally never date, because they want to fill the loneliness void. The problem is that, although the loneliness may be cured, being with the wrong person can open up the door for other issues such as a loss in trust, neglect, or stress. People are not the cure to loneliness; the cure is finding comfort in being alone.

I will never tell you that you have to like being single, but I will say that you have to love yourself more than you hate being single. When your hate for being single outweighs your love for yourself, you are more likely to settle and end up in an unhealthy relationship. But when you love yourself unconditionally, you will be willing to do whatever it takes to protect yourself from being devalued by another person. Make sure that you become comfortable with being single before you begin to date; this way, you will not settle.

Low Self-Value

When a person does not have a full understanding of themself and their value, they are vulnerable to predators who try to define their value for them. For instance, if a person feels they are not relationship material, they will more than likely never end up in a committed relationship. This usually results in these individuals becoming stuck with a person who never gives them a title but monopolizes all of their personal resources (time, energy, emotions, sex, money, etc.) without giving them any form of commitment. The consequence of this type of relationship is people feeling even more devalued, causing their self-esteem to plummet.

Since you are reading this book, I will assume that you are looking to be in a solid relationship with the hopes of settling down. If this is the case, you must make sure that you are at a point where you fully value yourself before dating. You must know that you are worthy of being purchased and not rented. Now the term "purchased" may sound a little weird, but it is a metaphor for saying that you must see yourself as a long-term investment instead of a short-term investment. Let me explain this philosophy using cars.

When a person rents a car, they temporarily use the car to fulfill whatever needs they have at that moment and return it after they are finished. The result of people consistently renting and returning a car is that it experiences wear and tear, its mileage increases, and its value constantly goes down. Similar to this thought, some people use others for their temporary pleasures and return them back to the dating pool after fulfilling their desires. Unfortunately, being used and returned to the dating pool has negative effects on a person, because it causes their perceived value to lower each time they are taken for a ride. Their number of sexual partners rises, and the wear and tear from the emotional roller coaster of unhealthy relationships decreases their self-esteem. This usually results in a person finding it hard to find someone who is willing to put a long-term investment into them.

This is completely contrary to the process of purchasing a car. When a person purchases a car, they go through a credit check to prove they can handle the payments, and they are forced to decide whether they are willing and ready to invest in the car, due to the large amount of money they must spend to get it. This is the same for people who value themselves. They put interested individuals through a "credit check" to make sure the person is worthy of having them, while also making sure the person is ready, willing, and able to make a full investment into them for the long term.

The story you just read illustrates the importance of knowing your value. If you see yourself as a "rental," you will be rented and returned, but if you view yourself as a "purchase," you will only accept serious inquiries. It is imperative that you know your value and have strong self-esteem prior to dating.

Apology

I have learned over the years that many times a simple apology would help some women find closure to their negative situations. The problem is that many guys are too egotistical and have too much pride to apologize and admit that they did anything wrong. This results in women being damaged and upset forever because they never got the apology they felt they deserved.

Although I am not the guy who hurt you, I would like to apologize on behalf of any man who has done you wrong. I wrote this poem after I got hurt and realized the pain I inflicted on women when I was young and immature. I hope you can accept this poem as an apology from me on behalf of the guys who did you wrong, so that you can move forward in life and become the queen God designed you to be.

The Apology

Dear Beautiful Queens,

We apologize for the hurt, the pain, the sweat and the tears
We apologize for the drama, the neglect, and the abuse over the years
We apologize for the lack of love, the lack of trust, the lack of affection that wasn't given
We apologize for the time you lost by trying to make us happy, instead of you just living

We apologize for the false promises we made to make you think that it was more
We apologize for not treating your body like a temple, but instead treating it like a whore
We apologize for intentionally causing arguments and intentionally causing drama
We apologize for NOT making you our wives, but instead making you our "baby mamas"

28

We apologize for allowing you to be promiscuous when we knew that it was wrong
We apologize for overlooking your true beauty within, for the pleasure of seeing you in a thong
We apologize for seeing you as a piece of meat instead of seeing you for who you really are
We apologize for leaving you at a lower level instead of helping you raise the bar

We apologize to your father for taking the innocence away from his little Queen
Knowing that he's in denial about his baby growing up and thinking that she's still clean
We apologize to your mother for the hurt and pain during labor she had to endure
Her precious little girl has now grown up and we're the reason she's no longer pure

Last but not least, we apologize to our Lord and Savior for not living by His precious Word
If we would have allowed God to lead our life, none of this would have ever occurred

Sincerely, Apologetic Men

Now that you have hopefully accepted the apology and are whole or on a path towards completely healing, I would like to use two metaphors that will encourage you to hold yourself to high standards while also holding men to high standards. The first metaphor is, "Be a Queen and NOT a Jester," and the second is, "Be a Treasure NOT a Prize."

Be a Queen and NOT a Jester

When I think of a queen, I think of prominent women such as Nefertiti, Queen Elizabeth I and II, and Cleopatra. In popular media, I think of fictional characters such as Queen Aoleon from the hit movie *Coming to America*. These ladies were considered royalty in their native lands and received the utmost respect from others.

In American culture, we do not have royalty, but in some subpopulations, the term queen has been used to identify women. Particularly in the African American community, it is fairly common to hear the term *beautiful Black queen*. There could be a number of reasons for the use of this terminology in these subpopulations, but it is ultimately supposed to have a positive connotation associated with it.

What is a Jester?

Jester is another name for a joker, prankster, fool, and buffoon. During a game of Spades, the joker cards are sometimes included and considered the most powerful cards in the deck, even more powerful than the king and queen cards. This is completely opposite of the real-life hierarchy of the royal kingdom, in which jesters are on the bottom of the totem pole.

The true role of a jester in the royal system historically was to entertain the royal family by doing humiliating acts. Jesters dressed in eccentric hats and clothing to draw attention from royal families so they could be selected by the king and queen to perform. In today's society, the words *jester* and *buffoon* refer to people who amuse others in a humiliating way.

Why "Be a Queen and not a Jester"?

I strategically chose this parallel because I feel it relates to modern-day dating and relationships. I have counseled a lot of women in their dating situations and noticed that most women I counseled were functioning in the capacity of a jester by trying to entertain and appeal to men, instead of functioning as queens and being treated as royalty.

It is my belief that all women were designed to be queens and are supposed to be treated as such. The problem is that society and circumstances have instilled in us the belief that women are subpar to men and are supposed to prove themselves as being worthy or valuable. This is evident in many different facets of life, such as corporate America (glass ceiling effect), religious institutions (women have no place in the pulpit), and popular media. This notion that women are subpar and should function in the role of jesters is heavily conveyed in music videos, which generally showcase male artists surrounded by a group of "thirsty" groupies who appear to be chasing them. These images symbolically portray guys as kings, while the women are playing the role of jesters, trying to prove themselves worthy of being with them.

Modern-Day Queens

A modern-day queen is an individual who fully respects herself and does not allow others to disrespect her. These are women with class who know their worth and do not settle for mediocrity. These women are seen as more than their physical presence and are respected because of their inner beauty.

Although America does not have a royal hierarchical system, there is one particular woman in my mind who stands out as a modern-day queen. This person would be none other than the beautiful First Lady Michelle Obama. When Michelle Obama walks into a room of people, she automatically draws attention. The attention drawn is not a result of the clothes she wears nor the shape of her body, it is more about her confidence, classiness, and ability to give off the vibe that she knows her worth. I find it hard to believe that anyone would ever approach Mrs. Obama disrespectfully, because it is hard to disrespect value.

Another factor that suggests that Mrs. Obama is a modern-day queen is the way President Obama treats her.

Sometimes, when President and Mrs. Obama are on camera and he looks at her, there is a sparkle in his eye that insinuates that she is a woman of value and that he is proud to call her his wife. This is what it means to be treated as royalty and treated with the utmost respect, because not only do others respect her, her husband also respects her. Michelle Obama is not the only modern-day queen. There are examples of these beautiful women all over the country. Some of your mothers, grandmothers, teachers, mentors, professors, and acquaintances from your communities are living examples of royalty.

Modern-Day Jesters

We are bombarded with modern-day jesters every day in the media. From reality TV shows to "tell-all" books, we see women who are lowering their standards and taking the role of jesters. It saddens me when we see young ladies in their late teens and early twenties seeking attention by fighting over men who are twice their age on popular reality shows. It further saddens me to see women glamorize the meaning of the term *groupie* by writing books about their sexual encounters with married professional athletes. On other shows, women exploit their failed marriages to professional athletes but further degrade themselves by sleeping with different athletes every episode.

These shows are the epitome of the term *jester*, because in all of these shows and books, the males are put on pedestals because they have women on national television chasing, having sex, and fighting over them. The problem is that this ultimately leads to women getting a bad reputation, and a message is sent out to young women that the role of a woman is to be a jester.

Beyond popular media outlets, women functioning as jesters are also seen in everyday life. For example, guys are labeling women as their "number-one woman," as if he has a starting lineup in a game of basketball; sadly, some women see this as a compliment. In other situations, men are sleeping around on their girlfriends and wives and are not being reprimanded for it, ultimately leading to these women being damaged and hurt. There are other instances where women are accepting being "friends with benefits" whenever a guy does not want a relationship and end up getting hurt when he cut ties with her to get with the woman he ultimately wants to be committed to.

For these reason, I highly encourage you to focus on viewing yourself and functioning as a queen and not a jester. This can be accomplished using the next metaphor.

Be a Treasure NOT a Prize

I am a firm believer that women should strive to be treasures and not prizes. Why?

1. **Treasures are found, and prizes are won.** When I look at reality shows, music videos, and most things in the media, I see a lot of women who are "prizes" that guys choose from. In reality shows, these prizes are in the form of a group of women vying to be chosen by a famous guy. In these situations, the guy gets to choose his prize woman from the pack. In the "real" world, this is in the form of women sleeping with guys, fighting other women, and/or expending their time, energy, and emotions trying to prove to a guy that they are worthy of being the special one.

Conversely, treasures do not have to be chosen or do any extra work to stand out. Treasures are typically found through hard work and careful planning. In today's world, treasures are beautiful women like our First Lady, Michelle Obama. President Barack Obama discussed how it took him multiple attempts to get his treasure and it did not come easily. This is because the First Lady viewed herself as a treasure and required President Obama to work diligently to prove that he sees the true value in her.

2. **Prizes are won playing games, and treasures are found using maps.** If I wanted to win a stuffed animal at an amusement park or the money pot in a game of poker, it would require me to have a certain skill to become the victor and collect my prize. In today's society, it seems that if guys obtain skills in the area of swag, talk game, and learn to play off of the insecurities of women, it is really easy for him to win and collect his prize, which is usually a woman with whom he is not "technically" in a relationship, but who gives him all of the perks that a husband should be receiving. This is evident in the fact that a lot of women end up sleeping with guys in a matter of weeks, and when he finally tells her that he does not want to make a commitment to her, she is willing to stay around because of the investment she has already put in.

When I say that a map is required to find women who are treasures, I mean that there is a certain way to gain access to these women's minds, bodies, attention, and emotions. Acquiring these things typically happens through stages. For instance, if you watched the *National Treasure* movies or any other movies that required people to use maps to find treasure, you will notice that there were various steps that had to be completed in order to find the treasure, and they generally required a lot of work. Women who are treasures make guys work hard for them and require these men to go through various stages before gaining access to them. This access is gained through proper courting, guys displaying consistency by having their actions align with their words, and sex being seen as sacred and not "just something to do."

3. **Prizes are in abundance and are temporary, but treasures are rare and last forever**. If I won some quick money in a game of poker, that prize is only as good as the amount of time I have the money. Once I spend it, the money is no longer of any value to me, and the items I purchased are what become valued. We can relate this to women. If a guy won a woman for the reasons listed in #2 and she is his prize, once he uses (spends) her and gets everything he can (sex, money, energy, time, etc.), then she is no longer of any value to him. He can move on to the next one, because there is an abundance of other women who are similar to her with whom he can repeat the cycle.

   On the other hand, treasures are forever and rare. If a coin collector heard that there was a rare, limited-edition coin that was worth a large amount of money buried in a park, but it would require a lot of work to find, that coin collector would definitely put in the work required to find it. The important part is what is done with the coin once it is found. A person who sees that coin as having value would probably clean it, get it appraised, put it in a vacuum-sealed container, and handle it with complete care, because they would not want the coin to get damaged or lost. Similarly, a real man is willing to put in the work that is required to get a woman who is a treasure and make her his "queen and not his jester." After putting in the work required, a guy would be willing to take care of her, remain faithful to her, and handle her with complete care, because he will not want to hurt, damage, or lose her.

By no means am I saying that all men are dogs and that all men are bad. What I hope to convey is that there is value in women who see themselves as valuable and not a quick, cheap thrill. In conclusion, before you date, make sure that you have a healthy view of yourself and that you value yourself on a level from which no man can ever lower you.

CHAPTER 3

SETTING AND STICKING TO DATING EXPECTATIONS

One of the first questions I ask women when they express their desire to date is, "What are you looking for in a man?" There are two typical responses I get: they either do not know or they give the cliché statements that are very general and surface-level, such as, "I am looking for a man who will love me," "I am looking for a man who is cool," or "I am looking for a man who is ambitious."

For those women who have no clue what they want in a man, I try to explain that it is hard to evaluate a man when you have no standards or expectations to hold him to and that this could be a recipe for a disaster. This is like going to a car lot without a clue about what type of car you would like to purchase. If you have no expectations or standards, then the car salesman will try to convince you that he has a car that is the perfect fit for you, and you may fall for his sales tactics and end up with a car that is far from what you deserve. On the other hand, if you went to that same car lot with a specific car in mind and you knew the features you wanted it to have, then you would be less likely to change or allow the salesman to convince you that you should settle for a different car. It is important to set and stick to your dating expectations.

For the ladies who have cliché standards and expectations in men, I always challenge them to dig deeper and become a little more specific. I believe that dating is the first step towards marriage and that you want to make sure that you get what you desire, especially if there is a chance that you could end up marrying the person (scary thought, but it is a reality). Do not worry; I will help you dig a little deeper so that when you are on the dating scene, you will know what you desire in a man so that you will not settle.

The final question I ask people who are interested in dating is, "What do you bring to the table and can you meet the expectations that you set for other people?" In this chapter, I will give you a few tips on setting expectations and boundaries for potential mates to help assure that you are where you need to be prior to dating.

Do Not Set Expectations You Cannot Meet

Before we set your dating expectations for others, let's discuss you. There is an old saying about life that states, "You can't have your cake and eat it, too." In layman's terms, this statement means you cannot have the best of both worlds or you cannot have what you do not deserve. Over the years, I have encountered a number of people who set extremely high expectations for their potential mates. Although I believe in setting high standards and not settling for less, many of these standards set by people are standards they cannot reach themselves. This is called being a hypocrite!

A few common hypocritical expectations people set:

1. Demanding that their potential mate has a low number of sexual partners, while their own sexual history is pretty extensive
2. Demanding that a potential mate has money and a job, while they are broke and unemployed
3. Requiring that a potential mate be physically fit, while they are out of shape
4. Requiring good credit, while having bad credit themselves
5. Wanting a commitment from someone, while not wanting to give a commitment in return
6. Having kids, while wanting someone without kids

This list could go on and on, but the point is that there are some people who set expectations that they cannot fulfill themselves.

I believe that everyone deserves the best in a companion, but in order to get the best, you need to be the best. I challenge you to look at your life's situation and figure out what you bring to the table. If you realize you have a few areas that need improvement, take the time to focus on improving these things, so when you come to the table, you have more to offer.

I am not immune to this idea. When I was single, I had really high standards and required a lot out of the women I was pursuing. The problem was that I did not have all of my stuff together, and I was called out for being hypocritical. Once I went through my spiritual transformation and focused on bettering myself as a person, I realized I could have higher expectations, and this led to me meeting a woman who met my standards and whose standards I met – now she's my wife.

You will learn that my philosophy on dating is about you focusing on yourself and becoming the best that you can be. When you know you are at a high level, you will have high expectations for others, which will cause you to attract high-level individuals. This is a basic rule of the laws of attraction.

Creating Your Expectations

Expectations are the items on your checklists that you will use to determine if a man meets your minimum requirements for pursuing a relationship. This is like your computer requiring specific updates before you are allowed to run certain programs. If your computer does not meet the minimum updated requirements, then you will not be allowed to use the programs. This is how you should treat yourself. If a person does not meet your minimum expectations or standards, then they should not be able to have access to you.

Prior to dating anyone, you should form two levels of dating expectations. These are:

- Level one expectations – Negotiable
- Level two expectations – Non-negotiable

Level one expectations are those things you would like to see in a potential mate but are willing to compromise. For instance, you may prefer to date a man without children, but if he meets most of your other qualifications, you would be willing to accept the fact that he has kids. It is important to understand that whatever you choose to put as a level one expectation should be something that, if you compromise, it will not cause you to see the person in a different light. If a level one expectation is not achieved, it should never make you feel as if you are settling for less than you deserve.

On the other hand, *level two expectations* are those things you are not willing to budge on. Most level two expectations are those things that are a part of your core morals and values. For instance, if you are deep into your religion and would be bothered by dating a person who is from another religion, then you would make sure that religion would be a level two expectation.

I cannot tell you what you should put under your level one or level two expectations, but I can tell you that you need to think long and hard about what you choose. You want to make sure that when you start meeting people, you have a list of things that one must possess before they are able to have a shot at winning your heart. This is similar to the application process for colleges. They set minimum expectations and standards that prospective students must meet before they can have a shot at being admitted. You must have your own screening process.

Another reason you want to set these expectations is so that you will not allow yourself to settle or waver. While dating, you may meet a man who sparks your interest, but you later realize he does not meet your level two expectations. Since these are the things you say you would not budge on, one would expect that you would immediately turn him down. Unfortunately, human nature sometimes kicks in and causes you to lower your expectations to satisfy your flesh. I have seen this occur far too often, and the long-term results are usually not good. Having a reminder of these expectations will help you stick to your expectations.

Take some time to write down a few of your expectations. Do not take this lightly and make sure that you are realistic when deciding. This list is only for you to see, so be completely honest, so you can have a true understanding of what you expect from another person.

Level One Expectations – Negotiable

1. _____
2. _____
3. _____
4. _____
5. _____

Level Two Expectations – Non-negotiable

1. _____
2. _____
3. _____
4. _____
5. _____

Setting Boundaries with Titles

I have learned that a lot of dating issues occur as the result of undefined titles. These are situations where one person may feel they are headed towards a relationship, and the other person feels that they are only "friends." Things get even more complicated when the couple has crossed certain lines, such as intimacy and sex.

As a result of these complications with titles, I have created a plan with various stages for setting boundaries that could help you avoid the "titleless situation." This plan is about progressing but not moving too fast. At each stage in this plan, there should be incentives – more personal access to you – for making progression. This should be similar to job promotions: the higher your rank in an organization, the more access you have to confidential information. Please realize that progression should not be achieved without hard work. Here is my proposed set of steps toward effective dating using titles:

1. **Casual Dating** – This is when you meet, exchange numbers, and talk on the phone. At this point, you probably should not be in his home, nor should you allow him to come to your home. I would encourage you to meet with him in public locations. This will prevent you from getting into risky situations.

    Please do not become physically involved with him at this point. I can almost assure you that if you become intimate with him while "casually dating," he will not move forward with you, because it was too easy and too fast. You should also respect yourself enough to feel that no stranger is worthy of that type of access to you.

2. **Exclusive Dating** - After learning more about him and realizing that you would like to pursue more with him, you should move to the exclusive dating phase. It is very important that you make sure he realizes that you have moved to a point of being exclusive. At this point, kissing should be the furthest you should go. Contrary to popular belief,

setting these boundaries will force him to gain more respect for you, despite any attempts made to go further, even if he appears to be upset because he cannot gain more access to you.

During situations when he tries to go further, you should continuously tell him that you have respect for yourself and you do not think anything more than kissing would be appropriate. Guys who really like you for who you are will be completely fine with this, and it will make them respect you more, because you are probably different than most females they have dealt with in the past. Some guys will get upset and/or leave you, and you should see this as a caution flag, because intimacy should not be the basis for dating.

After exclusively dating for a sufficient amount of time, you should begin to have conversations about progressing into an official relationship. Both of you should have enough information and interactions to know if a relationship is something you would like to pursue. If it is not, then you both can part ways without you giving too much to him (emotions, the mind, or sex).

As stated earlier, there should not be any sex at this point in the dating process.

3. **Official Relationship** – Once both of you have determined you are ready to become a solid couple, you should transition into an official relationship. When a relationship becomes official, you should have an expectation that others will know about

your relationship. He should introduce you to others as his girlfriend and he should not be ashamed to be with you in public. Relationships are not meant to be a secret.

In regards to intimacy, I will leave it up to you and let you determine if you will allow it to be introduced into your relationship. For so many reasons, I think it is best to wait until marriage. Although these are my beliefs, I am realistic and fully understand that many people do not wish to wait that long. At least be at this stage before you allow yourself to engage in sexual activities with him. At this point, he has made a small promise to you – the relationship – which signifies commitment and exclusivity.

On another note, if a guy tells you that he is not interested in a relationship, you should respond by saying that you understand and you will keep it strictly platonic. You should make it known that friendship does not involve intimacy, exclusivity, or spending a lot of time together. I highly recommend that if it is only supposed to be a friendship, you limit the amount of time you spend with him. If you spend enough time with him and see his potential as a boyfriend, you could find yourself catching feelings for him, making it hard for you to avoid getting into a situation in which you never get a title. Remember that he stated he is not ready for a relationship, so any advances by him contradict what he stated he wanted: a friendship.

Low-Quality Mates Lead to Low-Quality Results

We live in a world where people buy items that are beyond their financial means so they can appear to have a certain status in society. This is in the form of women working tireless hours to be able to afford a pair of Christian Louboutins or men doing whatever it takes to buy a pair of retro Jordans. If you asked these individuals to buy cheaper or lower-quality shoes, you may escape with only getting cussed out, because I am pretty sure they would refuse to wear anything that was not of quality.

Contrarily, we live in a society where some women do the opposite in terms of dating. Instead of dating men of quality, many of them settle for low-quality men and date below their value. This is why we see successful women dating men who are doing absolutely nothing with their lives. The problem is that when you choose to settle for less quality, you risk being affected by the lack in quality.

For example, if you purchase low-quality…

- earrings, you risk getting an ear infection.

- furniture, it may only last a few years.

- car parts, you may find yourself stranded on the side of the road.

- cameras, you get low-resolution pictures.

Similarly, when you settle for a low-quality significant other, you risk having low-quality results in your relationship, and this could ultimately affect you. It is my belief that couples who are not on the same level will result in one person pulling the other person in their direction. Many people would argue that this is what happened to the late, great Whitney Houston.

Side note: By no means am I suggesting that the person you are dating has to make the same amount of money as you or they have to have a certain academic degree. What I mean is that they should be working toward similar goals, they should be equally yoked spiritually, and they should have similar drive and ambition.

The bottom line is that we have to treat our relationships similar to the way we treat material things. We have to set high standards and not waver on them. If you end up with a lower-quality person, you may end up with low-quality results and risk being scarred for life (heartbreak, depression, mental abuse, verbal abuse, drug addiction, STDs, etc.).

Avoid the Pen Pal Phenomenon

The 21st century has brought about wonderful changes in technology but created a "mess" in terms of dating. Unfortunately, I have seen an influx in the number of people "pseudo-dating" and a decrease in real dating. One form of pseudo-dating that has sprung into prominence is dating through text messaging. This occurs when the majority of the conversations are conducted through texting on an electronic device.

If you choose to use this dating strategy, you will become what we called "pen pals" back in the '80s and early '90s. What you would be doing is sending each other messages from a distance and waiting patiently for the other person to respond. Unfortunately, this method does not effectively build healthy relationships, and there are potential consequences.

If you are serious about building a solid relationship, you must not focus on pressing the keypad; instead, you need to focus more on using the phone receiver to talk verbally or meeting in-person so you can have proper verbal and non-verbal communication. Technology may have made it a lot easier to communicate, but everything that is easy is not always beneficial.

Chapter 4

IMPORTANT THINGS TO KNOW ABOUT MEN

There are many different books, YouTube videos, and other resources to tell you about men. Some of you have brothers, fathers, uncles, cousins, and friends who have warned you about men and tried to prepare you for these specimens from Mars. For some of you, the things I am about to tell you are nothing new, and others will be introduced to knowledge that may help you better understand how to interact and deal with men. Let's talk about a few of these things.

The Things that Make a Good, Dateable Man

If you watch the Lifetime network, you will see a lot of movies where, at the beginning, women meet men who appear to be perfect guys, but by the end of the movie, they realize the men are horrible and wish they never invested their time and energy into them. Unfortunately, this reality is not limited to Lifetime movies and occurs every day.

I am often asked what makes a man a good man. The term "good man" is a vague term that is quite debatable. A man can be a good man contingent upon the way he treats his kids, but that does not make him a great, dateable man. On the contrary, a man can be great in relationships but have no ambitions in life. I like to add the word dateable to the equation when we are speaking of good men, because most women want to know what type of men they should date. For the purposes of this section, when I say dating, I am referring to exclusive dating and not just casual dating.

In order to learn how to evaluate a good man, you must first know what makes a good, dateable man. In my humble opinion, a good, dateable man is a man who has proven to you while casually dating that he possesses characteristics that insinuate that he will make a great companion. I could write a dissertation on the characteristics that make up a good, dateable man, but there are some characteristics that are more important than others, and I will highlight them in this section. Please note that they are in no particular order.

1. **He will make you feel <u>secure</u>.** While you are dating a guy, you must evaluate the level of security you feel. Does he continuously reassure you that he will protect your heart and prove this through his actions? Or does he make you guess about his intentions toward you? While dating, some people are in situations that are like an unreliable car, where they feel it could break down at any time. In these types of dating relationships, there is no

sense of peace, and you are forced to always have your guard up. A man who is worth dating will make it his duty to let you know that you are special, you are the ONLY one, and you can trust him with your heart. The key is that these messages should not only be conveyed through talk; they should also be conveyed through his actions.

2. **He will make you feel <u>respected</u> at all times.** Respect is such a vague term and could mean a lot of things, but if you are being disrespected while dating, I am pretty sure you would know. No person is perfect, but at a minimum, you should always feel and be respected while dating. The truth is that if he does not fully respect you before you are in a relationship, then he will not fully respect you after you are in a relationship. Do not brush off and ignore the little moments of disrespect.

3. **He will be more concerned with learning about you internally than physically.** Men who are truly dateable will focus more on getting to know you internally than being physical with you. This is because they will feel they have just as much at stake as you do, because they are looking to make an emotional and mental investment in you. If a guy is always pushing the issue of having sex or if he always tries to steer conversations towards sex, then this is a caution flag, and you should be careful. From human nature, a good man may bring up sex, but it will not be at the forefront of every conversation.

4. **He will respect your wishes.** A good, dateable man will respect your wishes. If you say that you do

not want to have sexual conversations, he will respect that and will avoid having those conversations. If you tell a good man that you do not invite people to your home without getting to know them, then he will not push you to try and allow him to come over for a visit. The reality is that some guys will try to push the limit and bypass some of the barriers you set, because they want to see if you are bluffing or not. Good men naturally respect your wishes and work within the boundaries you set.

I do not want you to confuse this with him doing everything you want him to do, nor does this mean he is your slave and should jump when you say jump. What this means is that he will respect the parameters and boundaries you set around dating.

5. **He will be __consistent__.** Consistency is a huge part of understanding a man's character and it leads to a sense of security and stability. If a man cannot consistently treat you the way you wish to be treated or if he is unpredictable, then there is a good chance you would go into a relationship uncertain about who or what you might get. The actions of a man who is dateable will always be very consistent. His words will always match his actions.

Some guys can talk a good game, but their actions do not always align. For instance, if a guy tells you he will call you in an hour, then you should expect to receive a call in about an hour. If he cannot make the call in that hour, then he should at least communicate (possibly through text) that he will not be able to call you when he promised.

6. **He will not be afraid to talk about <u>progression</u>.** It is easy to start dating a guy, but sometimes it is hard to talk about the progression of the relationship. A good, dateable man will not be afraid of the progression conversation, because he will be intentional with why he is dating you. He will be vocal about his intentions for you and he will make steps towards proving to you that he desires to have more. Far too often, men tell women they are not sure about what they want, and they are not thinking about the future. I always ask the question, "What is the purpose of dating if you do not have the future in mind?"

7. **He will be <u>confident</u> but not self-absorbed.** A good man exhibits confidence and knows his value but he is not caught up in himself. He will realize that he brings value to the relationship but he will also recognize that you bring just as much value. A good man will never make you feel less than him and he will never make you feel like you should feel privileged to be able to date him. No healthy relationship is formed when people are selfish; instead, healthy relationships are formed when both individuals are selfless.

8. **He will be a man with a <u>plan</u> and will be working to fulfill that plan.** I do not believe that everyone has to be at the height of their careers or have the best job ever but I do believe they should have a plan for life and should be working to fulfill that plan. Quite often, I hear stories of individuals who state their plans but are doing nothing to work towards them. A good, dateable man will show you that he is

working hard to fulfill the vision he has set forth to accomplish. This may involve going to school or working on a business plan. I can assure you that a good man is not someone who sits around and moans and groans about not having a job.

9. **He will be able to <u>compromise</u>.** Compromising is a major component of a healthy relationship. If you meet a guy who is not willing to compromise, then you want to separate yourself, because the relationship will be one-sided. Good men will not have a problem compromising, as long as it is within reason. He will realize that everything cannot go his way and he will be willing to work with you to assure that both of you can come to a rational and logical conclusion.

These are only a few characteristics that are important when evaluating a man. While you are on social outings or when you are having daily conversations, make sure that you are evaluating him to assure that he is meeting these standards. When he does things that are contrary to the aforementioned characteristics, you should view these as caution flags. This does not mean that you should automatically quit dating him, but it does mean that you should be a little more diligent with assuring that he is worthy of continuing to date you. You do not want to overlook some of these important characteristics, because they could come back to haunt you in the long run.

Caution Flags While Dating

In the dating process, there are some things that men do that should be seen as causes for concern. I will share a few of these and give a few scenarios to give you a better understanding.

1. ***If you are still considered a friend, although you have crossed lines that most "friends" do not cross***

Scenario: You have been dating a guy for six months, you have shared tons of time together, and you have been somewhat intimately involved. The problem arises when you get around his friends or even strangers and he introduces you as his home girl … i.e. his friend.

People who are excited about you do not keep you a secret. If you are being kept a secret, then you may not be the "one." It is understandable if you just started dating and it is within the first month or so of getting to know each other, but after a couple of months, they should at least tell others you are dating.

2. ***If whenever you bring up the conversation about being in a relationship, he tells you that he is not thinking about that***

Scenario: Things have been progressing well with him, and you have spent a lot of time together. He butters you up to a point where you are feeling like you are gaining deeper feelings. You have been spending a lot of time together, and he has given you all of the signs that insinuate that he wants you to be the special one. Once you bring up the conversation about being in a relationship, he quickly shoots you down and tells you he does not want to think about that.

If a guy has given you reasons to believe that you are special to him, then why wouldn't he want to have a conversation with you about a relationship? Is the fact that you have spent countless hours with him and poured your energy and emotions into him not enough of a reason for him to discuss a relationship? The lack of wanting to discuss a relationship after the time, emotions, and sometimes physical interactions is a clear indication that you may not be the one for him, and this should be seen as a caution flag.

3. If the only time he calls you is when he needs something from you or he wants to try and have sex with you

Scenario: You meet a man who starts out by giving you a lot of attention. He woos and gets you to a point of being comfortable. You start being intimate with him, and things quickly change. Instead of calling and texting you a few times a day, he may only contact you once or twice a week. The problem is that when he contacts you, he is asking you to come over for the purposes of being physical, or he wants you to do something for him. Whenever you try to have a general conversation on the phone, he tends to be busy and say he will call you back (which is usually a text message saying he is tired and will contact you tomorrow).

When a guy is really feeling you and really wants to be with you, he will try to talk to you as much as possible. If spending time means that you are only having sex or doing something for him, this is a clear indication that you may not be the one for him and he is only keeping you around for the purposes of you catering to him.

4. If he tells you he is not looking for a relationship

Scenario: The guy you are interested in entertains your phone conversations, is intimate with you, and makes you feel special, but he tells you he is not looking for a relationship.

This is almost as simple and straightforward as it gets. "I am not looking for a relationship," translates into him telling you that he does not see you as the one. If you proceed knowing this information, then he can always tell you that he told you up front that he was not looking for a relationship.

Be Aware of the Guys Who Try to Make You a Fill-in

You will notice that I have written a lot about titleless relationships and, as you continue to read, you will definitely hear more about it. I am passionate about titleless relationships because a majority of the women I give advice to are individuals who are in titleless relationships. As optimistic as I would like to be for this type of situation and as much as I would like to see these women end up with a storybook ending, my mind always screams, "Fill-in!" One thing I have learned about relationships is that once a person feels they have met "the one," they do not hesitate to take the necessary steps to solidify the relationship.

Unfortunately, there are a number of men who have not found "the one" but feel the need to have a woman around to function in that role. This concept is similar to the way companies hire temporary workers. When a position is vacant, many companies hire someone to temporarily serve in that role until they are able to hire a permanent employee. In many cases, the temporary worker comes in and does the job, but they are released of their duties as soon as the company finds the person they think would make a better long-term employee. In relationships, this is a man keeping you around as a fill-in until he finds a woman to be his permanent companion.

I highly encourage you to take your time and properly evaluate a man, so that you can gain an understanding of his intentions for you. Most of the guys who try to make you a fill-in are interested in your time, energy, and most importantly your sex. This is why I am very adamant about taking your time before being physical with a guy.

Be Aware of the Breadcrumb Giver

Day after day, I counsel women who are upset because they give 100% towards a man but they only receive 25% in return. Typically, the 25% that is reciprocated does not contain any internal connections (spiritual, emotional, mental); instead, it is usually physical in nature. The overexertion of energy put into a person while receiving minimal effort in return is a formula for mental anguish and frustration.

While dating a guy, you must evaluate and make sure that he is not trying to give you only breadcrumbs. Dating was designed to be balanced, and both people are expected to give a 100% effort. Any time the effort percentages are not even and one person is giving more than the other, the situation becomes unbalanced.

There are men out there who only want to give you breadcrumbs, while expecting you to give them a full "slice." As with everything I have stated before, you must take your time and get to know who you are dealing with. A man who is a crumb giver can be recognized, because he will always try to make you chase him and expend your energy, while he gives you little in return. The ramification for allowing a person to eat well off of your full slice of effort while you are nibbling on breadcrumbs is you starving while they are being fulfilled.

Be Aware of Semantics

In the world of dating, a lot of guys have learned the art of semantics, and a lot of women have become the victims of this learned skill. In layman's terms, this means that a lot guys have learned how to structure their words in a way that allows them to get what they want from a woman without any form of commitment. This is very problematic, because what some women perceive as innocent statements are really intentional calculated statements that are very selfish in nature. To make matters worse, after things do not go as planned and the "situations" do not work out, the statements come back to haunt these women. This is because the statements were crafted in a way that typically leaves the women looking like the fools in a situation, and they are blamed for making the stupid decision of dealing with these guys, because the guys were honest and upfront with them through their semantics.

There are also situations where some guys do not use semantics (word play) but they say statements that are brutally honest and straightforward. There are some women who justify these brutally honesty statements by saying, "At least he is keeping it real with me," and they use this as their justification for proceeding with these guys. The problem arises when the desires of these women are different than what the guys have been honest about. These types of situations usually lead to unhealthy relationships, because some women feel that they can convince guys to eventually change their minds, and the odds of that happening are slim to none.

The Straightforward Statements

The great poet Maya Angelou once said, "If a person shows you who they are, believe them." She was referring to life in general, but this statement is true in the world of dating. I like to remix her statement and say, "If a guy tells you who he is, believe him." Many of the things that guys say are straightforward and do not take a lot to comprehend, but sometimes women give them the benefit of a doubt or they believe they can change his mind. As I stated before, once a guy has his mind made up about what he wants and does not want, it is very hard to change him. Below I will give you few statements that guys use that do not take much thought, but a lot of women choose to overlook the warnings and end up in unhealthy situations.

I am not ready to be in a relationship. When guys say this, they mean it. For guys, this is their warning to you, and they feel that if you proceed, they are not responsible for you getting hurt, because they told you up front what they did not want.

I see you as a friend. When guys say this statement, this is their polite way of saying they do not want a relationship with you. Although they took an alternate route of saying this, the statement is still straightforward because it clearly highlights that a relationship with you is not going to happen.

You shouldn't be dealing with a guy like me. This statement is pretty straightforward. If a guy thought he was going to be great in a relationship, he would never tell you that you should not be dealing with him. This statement is his way of telling you that he is not any good and that, if you proceed, you will more than likely be hurt by him.

Be Aware of Mixed Signals

This is where things can get a little tricky. Although the aforementioned statements are straightforward and you should take a man at his word, his actions could give you mixed signals. For instance, he may say that he sees you as a friend but constantly spend time with you, have sex with you, and give you attention. These types of mixed signals can lead to you trying to figure out if he means what he says. It is important to know that nine times out of ten, he still means what he initially said.

The reality is that this is a part of the overall strategy, and the calculated nature of the wordplay that some guys use. Guys know that if they continue to show women attention after telling them they do not want to be with them, the ladies are more than likely going to continue to interact with them. The purpose of the semantics were not to push a woman away, they were to set up an "out" for him whenever he no longer wants to deal with her. This way, when she gets upset with him for not moving forward with a relationship, he can say, "I told you my stance up front.'

Less-Defined Statements

There are other statements that guys may use that are not as defined as the ones mentioned above. These are usually statements that leave women confused about whether they should move forward with a guy or not. The danger in these statements is that they do not outright say that a guy is not interested, so there is room to believe that he may be interested in pursuing a relationship. A couple of examples of these less-defined statements are:

> *I am not sure what I want.* In my opinion, this is one of the most dangerous statements that a woman can hear while dating, because it leaves her in a position where she has to make the tough decision about whether she should continue to date a guy or not. If a woman continues with him, then he has the advantage, because he gets to choose if a relationship will evolve or not. If he chooses not to purse the relationship, then technically he is not wrong, because he never said he would.

> *I am trying to get myself together.* When a guy says this statement, he is basically telling a woman that he wants her time, energy, and emotions, but he wants to put the relationship piece on hold until he get himself together. The danger in this statement is, *what if he never gets himself together?*

The less-defined statements can create a lot of confusion, but you must approach these statements with a selfish approach. When they say they are not sure about what they want, then you must make sure that you do not give them access to you until they know what they want. You have to protect yourself. If you continue to give them everything while they are unsure about what they want, you risk giving them all of your most precious assets and them coming to the conclusion that you are not who they want.

Words of Hope

There are a group of words that some guys use in a very deceitful way that I like to call "words of hope." The reason they are called "words of hope" is because when they are said, they tend to give women a false sense of hope in thinking that a relationship has a possibility of forming. For example, I have told you a number of times in this book to look out for the statement, "I am not looking for a relationship," because it can come back to haunt you. Technically, this is a defined statement that is straightforward and does not require any translation to understand what a guy means. Unfortunately, some guys know how to add "words of hope" to this statement to make it a little more ambiguous and cause women to have a false sense of hope.

Instead of being straightforward, a guy may say, "Right now, I am not looking for a relationship." By adding "right now," the guy has made a relationship a possibility, and a lot of women are drawn in by the little chance of him wanting a relationship. This is similar to the mindset people have when they play the lottery. Although the lottery may seem impossible to win, a lot of people are willing to spend their money on the small chance they may become the winner, when in the back of their minds they know they will not win.

Dealing with These Statements

Healthy dating is not supposed to be confusing. If you find yourself dealing with these blatantly honest or ambiguous statements, you should see this as a reason to be concerned. Good men do not play games and will not lead you on. If a good guy says he is not looking for a relationship, he will not continue to pursue you and intentionally send mixed signals. If a good guy is confused by what he wants, then he will be willing to stop pursuing you until he figures out what he wants.

The sad reality is that there are a lot of guys who are not looking out for your best interest and are only out to fulfil their selfish desires. For these reasons, you have to hold guys accountable for what they say they want or do not want and, you must value yourself enough to remove yourself from them until they know what they want. The quickest way for you to become upset and really despise guys is to hear these statements from a guy and proceed anyway. Then, when things go downhill, he throws it back in your face that you are at fault for continuing when he warned you upfront.

Chapter 5

THE FIRST DATE

If you have made it this far in this book, you should be at a point where you are ready to actually date. We talked about all of the things that need to be in place leading up to the big day of your first date with a man. The time has arrived, and you are approached by a guy who wants to take you out. Now what?

When people realize I am a relationship expert, they tend to open up to me about everything pertaining to their dating life. Quite often, people come to me and tell me that they have met someone they are interested in pursuing and they are going on their first date. I always ask them, "What you are going to do for your first date?" A majority of the people tell me they are going to a movie, to dinner, or bowling. My second question is, "What do you hope to gain from this first date?" Most people say they are going for the purposes of having fun and to get to know a little about the other person. My opinion is that first dates are more than just a time to have fun, and I believe they are a time for you to weed men out using surface-level information. I would like to give you five tips to help you maximize your first dates.

1. Do Your Research Prior to Attending a First Date

People meet others in various places, such as clubs, churches, schools, through friends, gyms, the Internet, or in other random locations. Most of the time, these new love interests are complete strangers who you know absolutely nothing about. For these reasons, it is important to learn as much about the other person as possible before you go on a date with him.

You will be surprised with what you can find out about a person. Some men are sociopaths who appear to be respectable individuals. Others are individuals who have criminal records, but you would never know from their outward appearance. On the contrary, you may find out more information about a man that confirms he is a great guy.

Dating in the 21st century is far different than dating in previous time periods. Since most people like to share their lives with the world on social media, take a few minutes to Google your date's name. **This is not stalking. I repeat, this is not stalking.** Actually, this is you being proactive in gaining information about a person you are going to spend quality time with. In the same way you would research and do a background investigation on a babysitter to make sure your baby is protected, you need to research and do a background investigation on a person who you are about to spend time with. There are crazy people in this world, so I think it is only wise to gather as much information as possible.

2. Do an Activity that Forces You to Have Conversation

First dates are about getting to know basic information about each other, so it is important that you put yourself in a position where you can gather this type of information. It is easy to plan or attend a date that does not require a lot of thought, such as going to the movies or bowling. Unfortunately, these two activities do not create a lot of room for dialogue, and the focus is more on the activity than the other person.

If the purpose of dating is to get to know more about the other person, then you need an activity that will allow you to sit down and have an intimate conversation. I see a lot of women who settle for activities that do not require a lot of conversation, and they are left with a date that does not give them enough information to make a proper judgment about the other person.

Instead of settling for these cliché activities, I would like to give you a few suggestions for dates that generate conversation.

- A nice dinner at a restaurant
- Having a beverage at a coffee shop
- A walk in the park
- A walk through the city
- A jazz bar
- An ice cream date
- Doing a service project together
- Playing a game of pool

It is important to note that each of these date ideas generally requires you to be in a public location. You have to realize that your safety comes first, so you want to make sure you are not in an isolated area where something could happen to you. I do not intend for dating to be viewed as a scary thing, but you must be realistic in understanding that everyone is not honest and does not have your best interest at heart.

Secondly, when you have a first date in an intimate location such as someone's house, it could send the wrong message early on. The message sent is that you are comfortable with the other person and you are willing to allow them to enter your personal space. When evaluating a man, it is important to set boundaries up front by sending the message that he has not earned your trust and he is not worthy of your personal space. You want him to know that he has to go through steps to gain access to your personal circle, and this includes your personal space and attention. There is no reason you should have a movie night or hang out at someone's house on your first date.

3. Do Not Talk More than You Listen

Judge Judy says that we have "two ears and one mouth for a reason," and that is because we should listen more than we talk. First dates can be fun and exciting, especially if you find someone that connects very well with you. The overexcitement can sometimes cause you to become too relaxed, leading to you dominating conversations. If you are doing more talking than listening, then you will only gather a limited amount of information to use to evaluate the other person.

Effective communication is when both parties contribute an equal amount of dialogue. This means that even if you have the urge to continue talking, you will consciously back down a little to give the other person room to talk. The key is for both of you to learn more about each other and not the other person learning everything about you.

4. First Dates Are Not Times to Swap Life Stories.

Although you are evaluating the person you are dating and they are evaluating you, you do not want to give your entire life story on the first date. First dates are intended to be about surface-level information and not deep dark secrets. Your objective is to learn enough information to determine if you would like to pursue future dates. As more dates occur, you can begin to learn more and more details about the person you are dating.

Sample First Date Questions:

How was your day?
What are your hobbies?
What type of job do you have?
Do you have kids? If so, tell me about them.
Do you have any pets?
Do you smoke/drink/do drugs?
What is your favorite movie?
What types of foods do you like to eat?
What are your short-term goals?
What are your long-term goals?
Are you dating anyone else?
What is your favorite book? Why?
If you could live anywhere in the world, where would it be?
What types of music do you listen to?
What makes you smile in life?
Is there anything you are really passionate about?
What is your favorite quote?
Who is your favorite actor? Musical Artist? Sports Team?

5. First Dates Are Not Times for You to Get Wasted

Having alcohol on first dates is a debatable topic. I believe that certain alcohol is appropriate on first dates, such as wine, but I do not suggest taking shots or drinking strong drinks, such as Long Island Iced Teas or Mai Tais. In my opinion, you should be 100% alert and aware of what is going on at all times. If intoxicated or distracted, you could miss some important caution flags that could help you determine if you want to pursue more dates.

You should also be able to completely control your actions so that you do not say things that could make you vulnerable or reveal too much too soon. Sometimes alcohol can cause you to become too lax, and you do or say things that you end up regretting. I suggest that you save the heavy drinking until you have gotten to know the other person and you are at a point where you feel comfortable enough to be vulnerable around them.

6. Don't Spend All Night on the First Date

A great first date can be very exciting, and you could find yourself wanting to be with him all night. If you find him to be exciting and you notice he finds you exciting, it may be advantageous for you to end the date while you both are still full of excitement. This will help set up the opportunity for a second date on a high note. I also believe that cutting a date short sets boundaries. The message you are sending is that even though you may enjoy or appreciate his company, you respect yourself enough to not allow him to occupy too much of your time. Spending long amounts of time with you should be a privilege that he must earn and should not be granted on the first date.

7. Make Him Ask You For a Second Date

A lot of people will probably disagree with me on this tip, but I really stand by it. Since you are dating for the purposes of evaluating a man, you can gather a lot of knowledge about him if he asks you for a second date. By him taking the initiative to ask you for a second date, you can conclude that he wants to be around you again and that he enjoyed your company. It also sets up the opportunity for you to hold the power in the situation, because you will not be the pursuer and you will be the pursued. You hold the power, because you determine if there will be a second date and you control the progression of the relationship.

If it was the other way around and you asked him for a second date, he would have way too much information and he could use it against you. Most guys know that if a woman asks him for a second date, then she really likes him, and he can make her work to get with him. The ultimate goal is for him to work to get you, so make him man up and ask you for a second date. If he does not ask you for a second date, then view it as his loss, because you should see yourself as being valuable enough to be courted and pursued.

8. Do Not Do Anything Physical on the First Date

He may be cute, he may have sexy lips and a really nice body but the biggest mistake you can make is to do something physical with him on the first date. Physical does not only mean having sex, it also includes kissing, cuddling, or fondling. Lines are really blurred when you introduce physical elements into a relationship too soon. The goal is for him to get to know your mind and for you to get to know his mind. You also want to set the tone and establish boundaries by letting him know that certain perks (being physical) do not come without hard work.

9. It is All Right to End the Date Early

If you conclude that a person is not for you, you can politely excuse yourself from the date. I do not believe that you should have to torture yourself by staying on the date for the purpose of not hurting the other person's feelings. To be proactive with giving yourself an out from the date, you may want to establish a timeframe for your date before going on the date, such as an agreement to be out for two hours. If the date is horrible, then you will only spend two hours of your time. If the date is great, you can increase the time while you are on the date.

Chapter 6

THE PERFECTION PHASE

After the first date or even a few dates, you may realize that you really like the person you have been dating. You may be at a point where you talk all night on the phone, you may visit each other often, and there may be sparks in the air. The reality is that most relationships start this way, as I am sure that many of you have heard of the phrase "the honeymoon phase." This phrase is the cliché term used to describe the high levels of excitement that are present during the early phases of dating. Although this term is acceptable, I feel a more appropriate term is the "perfection phase." I choose to use the word *perfection* because, during this phase, the dating couple typically views each other and their forming relationship as being nearly perfect.

Although this phase brings great feelings of euphoria, there are a few areas of concern that must be addressed. The biggest concern is that during the perfection phase, a lot of people make relationship commitments because of the perceived perfections, but they fail to factor in the fact that the "high" created during this phase will eventually subside, and the imperfections will begin to surface. This is when people begin to realize that their new partner and relationship is not perfect and they start to second-guess their decision to commit.

A few common signs that the perfection phase is subsiding are:

- You do not want to spend as much time with the person, or they do not want to spend as much time with you.
- You start to see the little idiosyncrasies about the other person that annoy you.
- You do not compromise on things nearly as much as you did when you first met.
- You begin to move from little disagreements to arguments.

Almost all relationships will go through the perfection phase, but there are some things you can do to increase your chances of not making a premature commitment that you will regret. The most important advice I can give you is to **take your time**. To put the perfection phase in perspective, I will give you a personal story that parallels this concept.

> When my wife and I got married, our careers caused us to move from city to city, so we decided to live in apartments. The apartments worked for a few years, but we eventually wanted to move into a larger space that felt more like a house. This is when we made the decision to move into a

townhouse. While searching for a townhouse, we came to a property that looked spectacular. We did one walkthrough of the property with a broker and were sold on it. Once we signed the lease and moved all of our things into the property, we felt as if we were in heaven. As the days began to go by, we started to see the imperfections of the property and realized that there were a lot of things wrong with this place. This caused us to second-guess our decision to move into it. Cosmetically, it looked great, but the real issues did not come to light until we spent a decent amount of time in this place. Luckily for us, we were only renting the location, so we did not have to stay in the property for too long.

My wife and I constantly think about how things would have been different if we had spent more time inspecting the property before making a commitment to it. We put a lot of money into a place (paying rent) that we felt was not quite up to par. The sad reality is that the broker did a great job of selling the property to us, and she did a good job of making it appear perfect.

I tell this story because sometimes people treat dating similarly to the way we made our decision about staying in the townhouse. They make quick decisions, commit out of excitement, and fail to fully evaluate the person they are interested in. Later, they realize that the person is not who they thought they were. For these reasons, I highly suggest that you take your time and do not make a commitment too quickly. It is all right to enjoy a person's company and to be excited about the possibility of a relationship, but you must have a long period of evaluation. I cannot give you the exact amount of time that you need to evaluate, but I can say that you do not get to know a person overnight or over the course of a month. If the relationship is meant to be, it will blossom into something special, and you will have plenty of time to be committed, so again, I say, **take your time** and do not rush into a mistake.

I will address three other factors that one must consider during the perfection phase: the perfect alter-ego, overlooking red flags, and settling for potential.

The Perfect Alter-Ego

In my first book, *Through the Eyes of a Man: The Truth about College Dating Revealed to Women,* I introduced the term the "perfect alter-ego." The perfect alter ego is the flawless representation of self that a person presents to you while getting to know you. In layman's terms, this suggests that during the beginning of any relationship or while you are getting to know a person, they will put their best foot forward and strive to appear perfect to you.

This is an area of concern because, during the "perfection phase," you may never meet the totality of a person, but you still make your decision about settling down with them based on the fictitious person they presented to you. This can lead to a bad situation for you, because you will have built feelings for this person, making it difficult for you to leave the commitment even if the person changes. This is one of the reasons why there are so many people who are stuck with individuals they are not happy with.

The truth is that people can only maintain their perfect alter-ego for so long. The problem is that people tend to commit before the lifespan of the perfect alter-ego expires. As with the advice I have given earlier in this chapter, the only way to get to know a person is with **time**. I cannot stress enough the importance of crock-pot dating (slow dating) and properly getting to really know a person before making a commitment.

Overlooking Caution Flags

During the perfection phase, the blinders that we wear are in full effect, and our ability to overlook the caution flags are at an all-time high. Many of you probably have heard people refer to red flags, but I believe that there are more than just red flags. I believe there are green flags, yellow flags, and red flags.

Green flags are those little things that men may do that affirm that you should continue with them. These are the small gestures that show you that he is really interested in getting to know you and that he will treat you the way you deserve to be treated. Examples of these are:

1. He shows up on time.
2. His actions are consistent with his words.
3. Your core values and morals align with his.
4. He shows an equal amount of interest in getting to know you as you show him.

Typically, people use the term *red flags* for what I like to call *yellow flags*. These are small gestures that create some type of concern. The reason we call these *yellow flags* is because these gestures should cause you to slow down the pace of dating, similar to the way you would slow down for a yellow traffic light. Slowing down for yellow flags will give you time to evaluate him more closely to see if you should continue dating or if you should stop. Examples of these are:

1. He tells you he will call you at a certain time, but you do not hear from him the entire day or night.
2. He does not have a job and has not taken any steps toward getting one.
3. He consistently tells white lies, exaggerates, or omits certain things.
4. He shows small signs of being possessive, abusive, or manipulative.

Red flags are non-negotiable gestures that will cause you to completely stop dating a man. These are extreme gestures that do not require any evaluation and are grounds for you to instantly break off any ties with him. Examples of these are:

1. Physical, mental, or verbal abuse
2. Sexual abuse or assault
3. Core morals and values not aligning
4. No value added to your life

The examples given for each of the different flags are only examples. You have to determine what falls under the different categories. For some people, not having a job would be a red flag, and they would leave him instantly, but for other people, not having a job is not as big of a deal.

I would encourage you to never overlook the caution flags. Similar to the way you risk crashing if you fly through a red light in your car, you will risk crashing and being hurt if you proceed through red flags while dating. This is important because sometimes you will find yourself reasoning and trying to create logic for the shortcomings of a person, but that is only a recipe for disaster. There are tons of individuals who have sought my advice and admitted that they saw caution flags while dating but they overlooked them and paid dearly as a result.

Settling for Potential

Our human nature causes us to want to see the best in others, especially if we want them to be a part of our lives. If you are like me, many of you were taught to "give a person a chance," so when you see someone with potential, you jump on the opportunity with the hopes that they will eventually reach that potential.

> For instance, a guy may be physically attractive to you but have no ambition in life. A little voice in your head may begin to speak to you and say that you should still give him a chance because he may change and find ambition. Since you were taught that you should not be judgmental and that you should give people chances, you make the decision to pursue him knowing he does not meet your expectations. This is one of the biggest mistakes I see people make.

I am for giving people chances, but there are two things you should consider:

1. **A chance is synonymous with a trial period.** If you see aspects of a man that you like and other aspects that you do not like, you should take your time and "date" him but not quickly commit to him. Dating means that you are taking the necessary time to get to know him to see if you would like to commit. While dating, you must observe him to see if he improves in the areas you find lacking. At the

end of the trial period, if he has not improved, you must move forward, because if you choose to stay, you will probably always be bothered by his shortcomings.

2. **Just because you wish or complain does not mean he will change.** The rule is simple: people will change whenever they are ready to change and not because they are forced to change. Some may alter themselves temporarily to hush you up, but they will not fully change unless they see it fit to change.

Although I am for giving people chances, you must make sure that a man is worth a chance. If his flaws conflict with your ethical, moral, or spiritual values, you may want to stay, away because you should never go against your values. But if you find his flaws or his appearance or an idiosyncrasy annoying, you may be able to give him a chance to see if it is something you can deal with or if it is something he is willing to work on. Since I believe in not settling, I feel you should find someone who is a definite and not a possibility. Find someone who is equally yoked to you spiritually, emotionally, and mentally, and you increase your chances of finding a long-term relationship and not a short-term disappointment.

Chapter 7

LET'S TALK ABOUT SEX

There is a powerful drug that many of us are addicted to that is taking over our communities and having a negative impact on many relationships. To some, this drug is known as sex, to others it is called making love, and a few call it "f-word"ing. Regardless of what you choose to call it, I view it as the kryptonite to dating. Before going any further, I must say that when used properly, sex is a wonderful supplement to a healthy relationship, so please do not think that I am anti-sex.

When I describe sex as the kryptonite to dating, I am referring to the fact that once sex is introduced while dating, people tend to put less emphasis on creating a proper foundation for the potential relationship and more energy into getting their sexual healing. This leads to the dating process becoming stagnant, and the typical end result is an unsuccessful attempt at dating.

Sex Should Not be a Priority

Over the years, I have learned that a lot of people engage in sex very early while dating. The problem is that, once the sexual line is crossed, a lot of people fail to have full conversations anymore, and many of their interactions become based on physical relations. This is detrimental because, for any relationship to grow, there must be proper communication and a foundation set into place. You may ask, *what is this foundation?*

1. **Spiritual Foundation** – Both people must be equally yoked and headed in the same direction spiritually. Having a spiritual foundation creates the grounds for understanding each other's connection with God, moral values, and ethical values.
2. **Mental Foundation** – Both people must make sure that they are mentally in the same place. If two people are mentally at two different points in their lives, there is a huge chance that the relationship will fail. A part of the mental foundation is making sure that both parties are ready for a relationship and are willing to give 100% towards themselves and the relationship.
3. **Emotional Foundation** – Both people must make sure that they are emotionally invested in each other. Expressing emotions is a big part of setting a foundation, because it establishes trust.

The problem is that setting a basic foundation does not occur overnight, and sometimes it takes months or years to create. Unfortunately, a lot of people do not have the patience to wait this long to set a foundation and they feel compelled to have sex. I have noticed that some individuals make establishing their physical foundation a priority and view the other foundational elements as less important. The truth is that the physical foundation should be the last foundation explored, because once that line is crossed, the rest of the foundations are greatly affected. Remember that if sex is introduced too soon, there is a good chance that your relationship will never grow to be as strong as it could have been.

Don't Become "Just a Fulfilled Fantasy"

When guys first meet women, they usually notice their physical features and view them with a lustful eye. When I was younger, I can recall having a conversation with a few guys, and we joked about how we "started down and moved up." That is, when we met women, we start at their butts and then moved up their bodies, eventually making it to their face. I was definitely guilty of doing this, and, like a large number of guys, I always ended up viewing these women with a lustful eye.

Once guys create an image in their heads about what sex would be like with a woman, they will do whatever it takes to fulfill this fantasy. Guys' intentions for pursuing sex with women are not always to be disrespectful; sometimes they are looking to fulfill their own selfish sexual desires. Additionally, there are instances when guys may pursue women whom they are seriously interested in dating or making their girlfriend. However, when sex is introduced, everything goes down the drain, and he no longer has interest in her.

Think about this scenario. You are out with a group of your closest girlfriends and you see a Gucci handbag that costs $3,000. All of your friends wish they could have it. You like the bag so much that you decide you will do whatever it takes to get it. After working extra shifts and saving money for a few weeks, you raise enough money to buy it.

When you carry the bag for the first time, all of your girls admire it, and you feel that you have accomplished something great! You carry it for a few weeks, and, after everyone has seen it, it becomes "another one of your bags." At this point, you go shopping with your girlfriends again. While shopping, you see a Prada handbag that you and your friends absolutely love. Again, you do whatever it takes to get this bag. After working extra shifts and saving money for a few weeks, you earn enough money to purchase it. You carry the new bag for a few weeks, and, after everyone has seen it, it becomes "another one of your bags." And then this cycle continues.

When a bag becomes just "another one of your bags," you only pull it out every now and then. Eventually, you get completely tired of it, and it gets stored in your closet. You refuse to give it to someone else who may value it more, because you feel that it is your possession and you worked hard to get it.

Now, imagine that in that story, you are a guy and the handbag is a woman. Using this new scenario, I will explain the psyche of some men and their desire for sex.

A guy and his friends are walking in the mall and they see a girl they think is sexy. All of his friends talk about how fine she is and how they wish they could "hit it" (have sex with her). The guy finds himself lusting for her so much that he decides he will do whatever it takes to "hit it." After getting her number and making her feel special for a few weeks, he eventually has sex with her.

After doing so, he goes back and tells his buddies that he "hit it." His buddies are jealous of him and acknowledge that he has accomplished what everyone else wished they could have accomplished. This causes him to feel like a king for a few weeks, because she is sprung and he has access to her anytime he likes. After a few weeks of sleeping with her, the excitement of having this girl fades away and now she becomes "another woman with whom he has had sex."

A few days later, while walking in the mall again with a group of friends, he sees another sexy girl. Again, all of his friends talk about how fine she is and how they wish they could "hit it." The guy finds himself lusting for her so much that he decides he will do whatever it takes to "hit it." After getting her number and making her feel special for a few weeks, he eventually has sex with her. After a few weeks of sleeping with her, the excitement of having this girl fades away and now she becomes "another woman with whom he has had sex." This cycle then continues.

When a woman becomes "just another woman with whom he has had sex," she no longer has the value that she once had to him. At this point, he finds a new woman to have sex with, and his old sex partner is used periodically or whenever he is experiencing a drought. He is too egocentric and possessive to allow her to date other guys, because he feels he put in a lot of work to get her. He does just enough to keep her in The Circle, which you will learn about in the next chapter.

This story hopefully conveyed a message that once a guy has had sex with you and the lust has faded away, he no longer has use for you. Does this mean that you are no longer a good woman? Of course not.

Here, the guy placed value on these ladies based on their physical features and his sexual attraction to them. Once sex was accomplished and he had access to their physical features, their values diminished to him because he had fulfilled his fantasy. Since he saw no other value in them to keep him interested, he moved on to the next woman.

Save Sex

Because of my spirituality, I am a strong believer that sex should be withheld for the person you intend to marry. Although I think this message is an ideal one, I know that it is not necessarily realistic for a lot of people. For those women who wish to engage in sexual relations, I highly recommend that you do not introduce sex into your relationship until a man has demonstrated that he has fallen in love with your inner person.

When guys first meet women, we build up a desire for them physically and sexually, and it becomes the value we place upon them. For example, when a guy sees a woman with a nice body and a beautiful face, her physicality is all she is worth to him at that moment, because that is what drew him to her. He has not had time to get to know her internally. Since this is the value placed upon her, he hangs around and shows interest in her based on this physical and sexual value. Once he engages in sex with her, her value declines because his desires have been fulfilled. This is similar to the handbag scenario. The girl wanted the handbag so badly that she did whatever it took to get it, but when she finally got it, the desire started to fade away. This concept is very important for you to know, because once the value a guy places upon you begins to fade, so will his interest, primarily because he has no other reasons to value you.

If a guy is held to standards that force him to get to know a woman prior to having sex with her, and he subsequently falls in love with her, it is more likely that he will value her both externally (physically and sexually) and internally (mentally and emotionally). So in this scenario, if he had sex with her and his sexual desires were fulfilled, causing her sexual value to diminish, he would still value who she was on the inside, which would more than likely result in him not walking away from her so easily.

The key is to set boundaries that make a guy get to know you and fall for you as a person rather than what you can do for him physically or sexually. After engaging in sex, guys often ask the question, "Why would I waste my time getting to know her if she has already let me have sex with her?" Truthfully, once sex is introduced into the situation, many guys only want to be around you and do things that would ultimately lead to sex. Another mistake is that I have seen so many women use their looks and talk about how great they are at having sex as a means to attract guys. The truth is that good-looking women and great sex can be replaced overnight. There are tons of beautiful women who are good at sex. Men do not fall in love with sex or looks. Your looks and sexual abilities will only get you so far because over time, those things will diminish.

Contrarily, when a man falls in love with the internal being of a woman, he finds it hard to let go of her. When a guy finds what he thinks is a great woman, who usually has a great personality, a bright future, and a great deal of self-respect, he will do almost anything to keep her, because she is very hard to replace. I encourage you to be a woman who has value beyond her physical features and sexual ability. If you want a great man, you have to show him that you are a woman of internal value.

Please remember that this is not only about you proving yourself to a man. He must be able to prove that he has what it takes to have access to your inner being as well, including showing a true commitment to your internal value before he is allowed to experience your physical value. A man who truly values you will support you in your endeavor to abstain from sex. If you feel that you need to consent to sex to keep a man around, I can promise that this guy is not the guy for you.

Test Driving

I meet a lot of people who state that it is important for them to "test-drive the goods" before they can make a decision about being with a person. They feel that they need to explore the other person sexually, because they do not want to end up committing to a person who cannot perform well in the bedroom. I do not believe in this philosophy and I believe that great sex is the result of a solid foundation and connection.

Test-driving is only for cars, not relationships. The problem is that when you allow someone to test-drive you, they have FULL ACCESS to you with the OPTION OF LEAVING. This is basically giving your goods away for free and getting nothing in return if the other person determines that you are not worth it. Instead of allowing someone to test-drive, make them research and evaluate you for the sake of determining if they want to be with you. They should want to be with you for all of your internal traits and not for your sexual ability.

The 90-Day Sex Rule

At almost all of the seminars or panels I am a part of, I am asked about some of Steve Harvey's advice. Like many of you, I watched Steve Harvey's movie, *Act Like a Lady, Think Like a Man*. Before anyone calls me a hater, I will say that the movie was funny and very entertaining. I will also go on the record and say that some of the standards that Steve suggests that women should set are good standards. There was one particular section that I would have to disagree with Steve on, which is **the 90-day rule**.

If you have not watched the movie or read the book, Steve suggests that women should wait 90 days before "giving up the cookie" (i.e. have sex). The thought is that a man should go through a probationary period before he gets the benefit of having sex with a woman and, during that probationary period, he should prove himself to this woman. Since I have been in the profession of giving relationship advice, I have been very cautious about asking women to set a timeframe for having sex with a man, especially if they are going to tell the guy the amount of time it takes to have sex with them.

As a man, if a woman told me that she has a 90-day rule for having sex, I would plan accordingly to make sure that I am around for at least 90 days. The problem is that making a guy wait 90 days is not an indication that he wants to be the special guy in her life, and there is no promise that he will be with her after having sex. For some men, they see 90 days as a challenge and get a thrill out of working to break her. If he fails to break her within 90 days, he will still feel victorious because at 90 days he knows he will get what he ultimately wanted — sex.

What I Propose

Although I did not follow God's formula and had sex prior to marriage, I will say that I am a huge advocate for waiting until marriage before having sex. Some may call me hypocritical, but I know that sex ruined many potential relationships that I had prior to inviting God into my life. Once I found God, sex dropped on my priority list, and I started caring more about the spiritual development of a woman, her emotional stability, her goals and ambitions, and other characteristics that were internal. This caused me to seek my queen for more than sex, and I did not need a 90-day rule.

I am realistic in knowing that the average person feels they cannot wait until marriage to have sex. I would propose that instead of setting a 90-day rule, set standards and create a solid foundation before opening sexually to a man. Examples of these standards are:

1. Have a commitment from him, not only through words but through actions.
2. Have a title instead of a promise. Sometimes guys can make vague statements to make you believe

that your interactions will turn into a relationship, such as, "We will see where this situation will go."
3. Make sure he displays love through his actions and not his words.
4. Make sure you have more than a secret relationship, meaning that more people know about your relationship than the two of you.
    *These are only examples of standards.

In my opinion, 90 days is not enough time to get to know or evaluate a person. Some would even argue that at day 90, you are still in the "perfection phase," so you still have not met the real person yet. As I have been saying throughout the entire book, I believe that establishing **a solid foundation** is a lot more important than a 90-day rule. I really encourage you to take your time and focus on foundation and not time. If a guy feels that you are worth the wait, he will wait as long as he needs. If he cannot wait, then it will be his loss and not yours.

Physical Health

When we speak of healthy dating, we are also speaking about your physical health. Since sex appears to be a popular subject that generates a lot of discussion, a lot of relationship experts do not like to speak about the negatives of sex, because it is not as exciting and it sometimes pushes people away. This is like pastors who choose to only preach about Heaven but avoid speaking about Hell because it scares and pushes people away. I feel obligated to speak to you about some of the realities of sex, even if they are not popular to discuss.

I cannot tell you the number of times people have confided in me that they have been diagnosed with an

STD they contracted from a person they were dating. One of the first questions I always ask them is, "Did you get tested before being sexually active with the other person?" Over 90% of the people I asked this question to admitted that they never got tested.

Although I highly advise you to wait to have sex, I am a realist and I realize that people are going to have sex. If you are going to have sex and cannot control your hormones, my first advice is to please get tested and have your partner tested. I have realized that a lot of people are afraid to ask others if they have been tested. My theory is that if a person gets defensive when you ask them about whether or not they have been tested, it is something triggering their defensiveness. This defensiveness could be caused by a person knowing they have an STD, or the fact that they really do not know their status at all and are scared to find out.

My second piece of advice is that the terms "dating," "exclusive", and "relationship" are not cures for an STD. Sometimes people feel that once they establish some type of relationship, it is an automatic pass to have sex and, in some cases, have unprotected sex. Unfortunately, there are some STDs that are not curable and, regardless of how much you get to know a person or how much time you spend together, their STD is not going anywhere, so it is wise that you both gets tested together before doing anything sexually. This simple statement carries a lot of weight: "A few minutes of pleasure can lead to a lifetime of misery."

Chapter 8

THE CIRCLE

Initially, I wrote this chapter for my book to college students titled, *Through the Eyes of a Man: The Truth about College Dating Revealed to Women*. The response from this chapter was so great, and the women felt it helped them so much that I decided to include it in this book. This chapter is very important, and I pray that it will help you avoid being caught up in what I describe as "The Circle."

The Circle is my way to illustrate the psyche of some men while dating. When I am giving presentations at various institutions, conferences, and seminars, The Circle is typically the highlight. It is my hope and prayer that this chapter helps you either avoid getting in The Circle, or gives you enough enlightenment and empowerment to get out of The Circle. Over 90% of the women who come to me for advice are caught in The Circle, and it is disheartening because their lives are put on hold for guys who do not treat them with respect. I am definitely guilty of using The Circle when I was young and immature, and I will make sure that I explain it to you in full detail, because I do not want you to become a victim.

What is The Circle?

The Circle is a strategy used by men to keep women around, regardless of the circumstances surrounding their relationship. It is not only limited to official relationships. It is also used when individuals are talking, dating, or are friends with benefits.

The Circle is broken into four levels: "Sprung," "Feeling Neglected," "Considering Leaving," and "Danger Zone."

The Circle from a Woman's Point of View

The Sprung Stage

While hanging out at the mall, a lady is approached by a man. He tells her that he has been watching her and finds her to be very attractive. He states that he would like to get to know her better and possibly take her out. He asks for her phone number, and she gives it to him. When she gets home, she notices that the guy sent her a text message expressing how he really enjoyed meeting her.

She responds to his message, and for the next few days, they communicate via text message.

After a few days, he tells her he wants to call her. They begin having long verbal conversations on the phone, going into the wee hours of the morning. She thinks he is fun to talk to and really attentive, and she likes that he always has things to discuss during their conversations. After days of talking on the phone, she feels comfortable enough to allow him to visit her home.

As time progresses, he constantly reassures her that he is different from other guys and that he will not hurt her. From her perspective, his actions align with his words and he makes her feel special. Thus, she begins to fall for him because he appears to be the perfect catch and he is noticeably different than the other guys she has dealt with in the past. This realization causes her to let down her guard and to start opening up herself to him emotionally (telling him how much she likes him), sexually (having sex with him), and mentally (constantly thinking about him and wanting to be with him all the time). She also begins to tell her friends how wonderful he is and how she thinks he may be "the one."

The Feeling Neglected Stage

After about a month of being with him and experiencing pure euphoria, she begins to notice that he does not do many of the things he did when they first met. The duration of their phone conversations and in-person interactions begins to decline, and he now appears to be busy all the time. She begins to question him about his changes, and he states that there is nothing wrong and that he has been overwhelmed with work and other personal matters.

She tries to be understanding and supportive because she cares about him, but she notices that he continues to go clubbing, hangs with his friends, and is constantly active on social media. This causes her to become suspicious because she feels that he has time for other things but has no time for her. This ultimately leads to her feeling neglected. She begins to question herself and tries to determine what she may have done wrong to cause him to want to distance himself from her. She tries to have discussions with him about her feelings, but he states that everything is fine and that he does not see a problem. As time goes on, his actions gradually get worse, leading to constant arguments.

The Considering Leaving Stage

With the lack of attention, constant arguments, and new suspicions of him cheating, she starts to seek advice from friends. Her friends assure her that she deserves better and that she should leave him. She ponders this thought for a few days. Deep within, she does not want to leave him, but she concludes that she has no other choice. At the point when she is about to leave – actually leave – or begins to talk to another man, he steps up his game and apologizes for his actions. He tells her that he has been dealing with a lot and that he did not intend to hurt her. He assures her that he will do better and that he really wants to be with her.

Back to Sprung

She ends up giving him another chance because, in her heart, she really wants to be with him. He stays true to his promise by doing all the things he did during the Sprung Stage. Again, she feels special and appreciated, causing her to become sprung again. This lasts for about three weeks, and then she begins to notice that he is starting to neglect her all over again. And so the cycle continues.

What Happened?

I am sure that many of you have been in a situation similar to the aforementioned story. The woman in the story above was caught in The Circle, which is a continuous cycle. She started in the Sprung Stage, moved to the Feeling Neglected Stage, considered leaving the situation, and right before she hit the Danger Zone, she fell all the way back into the Sprung Stage, causing her to start the cycle over again.

I would like to now show you how guys process The Circle using the same scenario. Hopefully, this will prove helpful.

The Circle from a Man's Point of View

The Sprung Stage

While hanging at the mall, a man sees a woman whom he has been watching for some time. He approaches her and tells her that he has been watching her for some time and he would like to get to know her. He asks her for her number, and she gives it to him. At this point, he knows that she finds him attractive, because he knows that no woman would give her number if she did not like something about him.

Once he gets back to his room, he immediately sends her a text message. In the message, he states that he enjoyed meeting her and he hopes she gets a good night's rest. The next day, he receives a response from her. He is excited because this shows him that she has some type of interest in him. They send messages back and forth via text message for a few days. He eventually requests that they move to a verbal conversation.

He spends many hours on the phone trying to prove that he really wants to get to know her. He makes sure he says things that make her laugh and keeps discussions going to make her feel comfortable. As long as she continues to talk to him, he knows that she is interested in him.

After he notices that she is comfortable with him, he starts making references to them possibly hanging out. He knows that he is in her good graces, so it is only a matter of time before she invites him over. After a few weeks, she invites him to hang out. This is huge for him, because this insinuates that her guard has lowered.

The invitation to visit assures him that she is really beginning to like him. He knows that she is somewhat hesitant, so he constantly reassures her that he likes her and has no intention of hurting her. She tells him about the ways guys have treated her in the past and that she has a hard time trusting men. He reassures her that he is different from other guys and he proves this to her through his actions. What she does not know is that he is only making sure to do the opposite of what every other guy has done wrong to her in the past.

As time progresses, he knows that she sees him as a great catch. This is evident because she constantly tells him he is different from other guys. After a few weeks, she begins to open up to him by telling him she really likes him. She eventually becomes completely comfortable with him and allows him to sleep with her. She starts to tell him that she is constantly thinking about him.

After sleeping with her for the first time, he knows that she has crossed a line that she probably would not have normally crossed. He realizes that she is having internal struggles because she has allowed a guy to sleep with her without being in a committed relationship. He apologizes to her for crossing that line and makes an agreement with her not to cross it again. He reassures her that he has no intentions of hurting her so she can feel some sense of comfort. He also tells her that he does not look at her differently, because he does not want her to feel as if she did something wrong.

He continues to visit and spend time with her and, "by mistake," they continue to find themselves having sex. What she does not know is that he recognizes she has sexual urges and desires, so when he makes moves on her, he knows that it is hard for her to control these desires, because she is vulnerable and really likes him. He knows that if they get intimate in any way, it would probably lead to sex. After a few times of having sex and reassuring her that he has no intention of hurting her, she becomes comfortable having sex with him. At this point, he knows that she is officially sprung.

The Feeling Neglected Stage

After about a month of having sex and spending time with her, he realizes she has really fallen for him and she has no interest in any other guys. He comes to this conclusion because she continuously tells him this. By now, he knows that she has invested too much in him to walk away, so he becomes lax when dealing with her.

Instead of spending time with her, he returns to doing the things he did before he met her. He starts going to the club again, being active on social media again, hanging with his friends again, and doing other things to occupy his time. Sometimes when she calls or texts him, he ignores her because he feels she always wants to be with him. He answers the phone sometimes, because he does not want to come off as a complete jerk, but during these conversations he tells her that he has been busy. When she asks him what has happened to cause him to change, he realizes that the easiest way to answer the question without hurting her feelings is to say, "Nothing is wrong." What she does not know is that deep within, he no longer sees her the same way he did when he first met her. He has accomplished everything – sexually, emotionally, and mentally – that he intended to accomplish. Truthfully, he no longer has any use for her outside of hanging out, having sex, or chilling with her when he is bored, because he does not want to be in a relationship with her.

At this point, he knows that she will do whatever it takes to try to be with him. He continues ignoring her as usual and he only visits her late at night so he can say they "spent time together." Night visits are good for him because it is a time when he can have limited conversation with her and have sex with her. She begins to question him about her feelings of neglect, but he continues to tell her that there is not a problem. He tells her that she is too sensitive. And on most occasions, this leads to big arguments. What she does not know is that the arguments are good for him, because they are his justifications for leaving her home or getting off the phone. When she is finished arguing, she is in her room upset and not functional. However, when he is finished arguing, he sees it as a way to be free from her for the duration of the time they are "mad" at each other.

The Considering Leaving Stage

He knows that he has been neglecting her by not showing her any attention, talking to other girls, and not making her feel special. He will not tell her the truth about why he has been neglecting her, because he promised her in the early part of their "friendship" that he had no intention of hurting her. Inside, he acknowledges that she is a good girl, but he knows that he does not want to be with her long-term. Although he does not want to be with her long-term, he does not want her to be with any other guys, because he is selfish. In his mind, he will do whatever it takes to keep others away from her.

He can tell that she is getting to the point where she is about to break. Her friends no longer talk to him, and she constantly tells him that she does not know how much longer she can deal with feeling neglected. Although she does not say it to him, he knows that she does not want to leave him because she has invested too much. When he senses that she is on the verge of leaving him, when she tells him she is leaving, and/or when she starts opening herself up to talk to other guys, he knows that he needs to step up his game so he can reel her back in.

The reason he wants to reel her back in is not so much about him wanting to be with her long-term; it is more so because he does not want any other guys to have her. He feels that he worked too hard to get her, and his ego causes him to feel as if she is his possession. For these reasons, he takes the steps to get her back.

He begins by apologizing for his actions. In order for her to take him seriously, he knows that he has to take the blame and admit to neglecting her. Because he uses her emotions as a means of luring her back in, he makes her feel pity for him by stating that he has been going through a rough time and has been really confused. He tells her that he has been having problems at work, his family has been going through some hardships, and about other issues that eventually cause her to feel sorry for him. He further says that he had *no intentions* of hurting her and that, if she gives him another chance, he will make it up to her.

Inside, he is fairly confident that she will take him back, because he knows she has **invested too much** into him to walk away so easily. As he calculated, she gives him another chance, and he takes advantage of this chance by doing all the things he did when they first met. He does these great things for about three weeks, until she begins to tell him that she is falling for him again. At this point, he knows that she is sprung again and is fully invested in him. This is his cue to become lax again and start distancing himself. And so the cycle goes on and on.

My Advice

The Circle is very real, and I have seen a lot of women get caught in it. The area outside of the *Considering Leaving* area is known as the *Danger Zone*. The *Danger Zone* is when a woman has made up her mind to leave a man and has no desire to return. A guy's primary goal is to keep his woman from making it to the *Danger Zone*. She may be allowed to flirt with the edge of the *Considering Leaving* stage, but he will do whatever it takes to keep her from crossing over into the *Danger Zone*.

If a guy is neglecting you and is not showing you the proper respect and attention you desire, I fully advise you to leave him. Do not give him a chance to go from the *Feeling Neglected* stage to the *Considering Leaving* stage. I am 100% sure that, during the *Feeling Neglected* stage, you told him that you were unhappy and wanted him to improve. If he could not get it right during this time, you should not waste your time with him.

What you have to realize is that the woman in the scenario met what she thought was a perfect guy. What she really saw was an alter-ego that he created to appear as the perfect guy. This creates issues because once he begins to treat her badly, she starts to reminisce about the alter-ego that he showed her when they first met. This is why, when a woman goes through rough times with a man, she states that she knows he is a good man and he has been a good man in the past. The truth is that the person she hopes he gets back to was really an illusion. She lives and stays in his circle with the thought that he will eventually revert to being this perfect guy. The reality is that it is nearly impossible for him to be that perfect guy because it was not his real identity in the first place. The true identity is the guy she experienced during the *Feeling Neglected* stage.

My ultimate recommendation is that you use the information in previous chapters to determine if a guy is really worth dating. This will be a proactive way for you to inspect him and make sure he is really interested in you for more than your physical features. Guys can only display their perfect alter-egos for so long. The problem is that many women give themselves to men so fast that they do not give the guys enough time to reveal their true identity. Please take your time, ladies, when dealing with men. Run a thorough ManFax report (bonus chapter) on him and make your decision based on the results.

Chapter 9

MOVING FROM DATING TO A RELATIONSHIP

You have made it to the last official chapter of the book and, at this point, you should be equipped with enough knowledge to date successfully. Given that I believe dating should be purposeful, there should be a point where you have to make a decision about whether to move forward and make a commitment or discontinue pursuing each other. The problem I see in many cases is the lack of progression while dating and people being left clueless about the status of their "relationship." This is why some people have been together for months or even years but have no true commitment or title. "Dating" should have an expiration point, and the couple should either progress to a commitment or part ways.

What is Commitment?

Dating is supposed to be about two people evaluating each other for the purpose of seeing if they are worthy of committing to one another. The problem is that the word "commitment" is often misunderstood, and people end up in unhealthy situations. Healthy dating is about grasping a true understanding of what it means to commit and building a relationship under this understanding. The term commitment means to entrust or commit to another person with confidence. When we take a look at this definition, there are a couple of words which instantly stand out: entrust and confidence.

Entrusting means to confer trust on. In layman's terms, this means that you give something to a person because you trust that they will take care of it. While dating, this is very important, because when you move from dating to a commitment, you are basically saying that you have evaluated the man and gained enough trust for him that you are willing to give him your heart, exclusive romantic attention, and a promise that he is the only one you want to be romantically involved with.

Confidence is a state of being certain that a predication is correct. I cannot count how many times I have met individuals who are willing to commit to a person they do not have full confidence in. These individuals were not fully certain that the other person was the right one for them, but they chose to commit anyway. Healthy relationships are formed when both individuals can be completely confident in each other. The best way to gain this type of confidence is through a slow and intentional vetting and evaluation process, i.e. dating.

When to Commit

The million-dollar question I am always asked is, "When should I move from dating to commitment?" In my experience, I have realized that there is no perfect way to tell when a commitment should happen, but there are some indicators that suggest the timing is right. Below are a few of these indicators:

1. When you feel you know the morals, ethics, and values of the other person and they align with yours
2. When you realize your goals and aspirations align with each other
3. When you move past the perfection phase and you appreciate the person even with their imperfections
4. When both individuals had ample time to evaluate each other and they both feel that the connection is right
5. When you feel that you can trust the person you are dating with full confidence to protect and fully value your heart and mind

When to Discontinue

Many of you reading this book have heard of the term "equally yoked." Most people use this term in reference to spiritual compatibility, but I believe the term refers to much more. As a practicing Christian, I stand firm in believing that you must be spiritually equally yoked with your partner; but as a relationship expert, I believe that you should be equally yoked in most core aspects of life. A few of these areas are:

Spirituality: attachment to religious values

Morals: principles of right and wrong in behavior

Ethics: a set of moral principles

Values: broad preferences concerning appropriate courses of action or outcomes

If you are anything like me, your spirit will not be settled if you are dating a person who does not share the same core values as you. I have personally ended a few relationships and have seen a lot of relationships crumble as the result of couples not being equally yoked in these areas. Figuring out if you are equally yoked with someone can be a long process, so it is very important to date slowly. Making a commitment to a person and later realizing that their core values do not align with your core values is one of the worst situations you can be in because your mind will be in conflict with your spirit. Your mind may tell you that you should continue pursuing the relationship, but your spirit will tell you that it is not right.

There may be points when you are dating someone and you realize that the core of them does not align with the core of you. What should you do? In this situation, I highly advise you to stop pursuing this relationship, because fundamentally the relationship is unequally yoked, and the odds of it surviving are slim. You may find yourself really liking the person despite being unequally yoked and you may even feel they will come around and become equally yoked in these areas, but changing the core of a person is really difficult to accomplish, because that is the foundation of who they are. The one constant I have seen is that when someone tries to change the core of another person, they typically burn themselves out and go through a lot of mental anguish because they expend too much energy on a lost cause. This would be similar to a mouse running on a wheel; although the mouse is putting a lot of energy into running, it is not advancing any further and will eventually tire itself out.

How to Bring Up the Conversation about Commitment

Bringing up the conversation about moving from dating to commitment tends to be difficult for some people. There appears to be a common thought that, by bringing up this conversation, one may push the other person away. I am a firm believer that, if you have spent a lot of quality time with a person and they were able to utilize your time, energy, and emotions, they should be able to have an honest conversation with you about the progression of a relationship. As I have stated many times before, the purpose of dating is to evaluate each other to determine if you want to move forward and commit to one another. This means that the discussion about progression should be a standard part of the dating process.

If you have been dating a person and have spent intimate moments together, given your time, and built emotions, and they get upset with you for wanting to discuss commitment, I think this is a caution flag and you should reevaluate them. You must ask yourself and the other person: What is the purpose of you expending your time, energy, emotions, and resources on them if they cannot express how they foresee the relationship progressing?

The reality is that some people are content with dating without a commitment. They want all of the perks of dating, but they do not want to discuss moving the relationship forward. These types of situations usually end up as quasi-relationships with an unwritten commitment. The commitment in these situations is based on obligation and not mutual agreement. The result is typically a relationship that is full of confusion, and the odds of it being healthy are slim to none.

The key to building a healthy relationship is to state your purposes for dating very early in your interactions. You must let the other person know that dating for you has a purpose and that, when you date, you will only continue if there is enough evidence to prove that the person is worthy of possible progression. Allow me to give you my testimony with my wife:

> When my wife and I first met, we realized that we had a lot of similarities. We were very excited about each other, but we both knew that the excitement was only good if we were on the same page about why we were interested in each other. One of the first questions she asked me was, *why was I interested in her and what would be my purpose for pursuing her?* At this point, I quickly realized that she wanted to make sure that I was not wasting her time and that I was on the same page as her about the purposes of us potentially dating. I told her some of the qualities that attracted me to her but I also told her that I was at a point in my life where I wanted to find someone to potentially settle down with. Naturally, I asked her the same question in return. She stated that she was not looking for a fling or to be friends with benefits; she stated that she would only date for the purposes of possibly establishing a solid relationship.

By having this conversation early on, we both understood the requirements for dating each other. Having this knowledge gave us the option to either stay or leave. Since we both agreed to start dating, we knew that the conversation about progression was going to come at some point. We did not have a problem when the conversation came up, because we were dating with purpose and both agreed early on that we were looking to date for the purposes of potentially progressing.

The worst situation would be you suppressing your feelings and desires of progressing a relationship for the purpose of not scaring the other person away. There are far too many cases where people allow themselves to be in titleless relationships because they feel they would offend the other person if they spoke of progression. The truth is that you should feel offended if the other person does not want to have that conversation, because at minimum you deserve to know the return on your investment.

Bonus Chapter

AVOID THE LITTLE BLACK BOOK

The *little black book* of numbers is a staple in male culture and plays a major role in the day-to-day dating activities of men. You may ask the question, *what is the little black book?* Historically, this book has been a private, journal-style book where men store the numbers of women they came into contact with; however, this book has transformed in the 21st century and is rarely in paper form. Today, the little black book is kept in a phone, computer, flash drive, or any other electronic device that saves data.

The purpose of this private book is to serve as an information hub and phone directory for men who wish to 1.) connect with women they are currently pursuing or 2.) reconnect with women of their past. This book is usually kept in a private place and locked so others cannot get access.

For years, these little books have caused major turmoil in many relationships, because a lot of women have found them and heavily questioned their men about the women who are listed in the book. The purpose of this chapter is to give you insight and a snapshot of the various types of women who are stored inside the little black book. This chapter is based on my perception, experiences, and talking to a large group of men, but it is not necessarily the representation of all men. Also, the descriptions you are about to read are not necessarily all of the women in the little black book, but these are descriptions of some of the most common women put in the book.

The Cool Girls

There are some people who would argue that it is nearly impossible for guys to be strictly platonic with women. In my opinion, there is some truth to this assumption, but there are a few instances where guys are strictly platonic with their female friends. In the little black book, we call these women the "cool girls."

The cool girl is the only completely innocent girl in the little black book. These girls are innocent because the guys they are friends with have no intentions of being anything other than platonic friends. As their name states, these women are cool, meaning they are cool to talk to and cool to hang out with from time to time, but there is nothing more to the friendship. Cool girls are usually treated and thought of as being like "one of the guys" or "a little sister."

The formation of this type of friendships happen in multiple ways. A few of these ways are:

1. Childhood Friend – Guys sometime meet "cool girls" when they are young, and the friendship grows over time. These friendships end up being brother-sister-

like relationships, and both male and female consider themselves as being family.

2. Not Attractive – Sometimes guys meet women they are not attracted to but realize that they are good people to be around. This could be a woman he meets at work or in school that he sees on a regular basis and has daily conversation with, but he never tries to pursue anything with her because he does not find her attractive.

3. Lesbian – Lately there has been an influx in the number of guys who have friendships with lesbian women. This makes complete sense, considering that guys and lesbians have the commonality of liking women.

Primary Choice

The primary choice is the best and number-one preference in terms of sex. These women are not necessarily kept around to start a relationship, but they are the first women called whenever a guy wants to fulfill his sexual desires. The reason these women are the primary choices is because they perform the best in the bedroom.

It is important to note that these women are not always viewed as hoes nor are they necessarily easy to get in bed. The nature of these women being primary choices is that they are sought after because of their ability in the bedroom. There are some cases where women become the primary choice after only having one sexual experience with a guy (i.e. he became sprung).

The Back-up Plan

Whenever a guy cannot have his primary choice to fulfill his sexual desires, he resorts to the women in his little black book whom he knows will be ready to fulfill his sexual desires. These readily available women are known as the "Back-up Plan."

Back-up Plans are ride-or-die women who do not ask many questions whenever a guy asks them to come over for sex. Most of the time, these women have accepted that sex is the entity that brings them together with a guy, and they are all right with this realization. With the relationship being mostly based around sex, phone conversations are scarce, and there are not many verbal conversations whenever they are with the guy. Sex is the only factor.

The Secrets

The secrets are, as their name states, "secrets." Secrets are women who guys make it a duty to keep a secret. There are a number of reasons why a guy may want to keep a woman a secret, but the one certainty is that he does not want anyone to know – not even his homeboys – about his sexual escapades with certain women.

A few reasons a guy may keep a woman a secret:

Unattractive – Sometimes, guys sleep with women who are not the most physically attractive, but they are able to satisfy them sexually. For these reasons, the guys may have an ongoing secret sexual relationship with them, but they keep it to themselves.

Women who are supposed to be off limits – Some guys have sex with women they know they are not supposed to engage in sex with, and they are forced to keep it a secret. This could be the ex-girlfriend of one his close friends, the current girlfriend of one of his close friends, the sister of a close friend, a friend of his ex-girlfriend, or anybody who he is not supposed to technically have sex.

I Missed My Opportunity

There are some instances where a guy has an opportunity to have sex with a woman and for whatever reason, the experience never happens. Some of these reasons are:

1. Right before sex was to occur, the woman felt guilty and backed out of it.
2. The guy did not have a condom on the night they were going to engage in sex, and she would not allow him to move forward.
3. Someone interrupted them right before they were about to engage in a sexual act.

Guys keep these women in their phones because they hope that at some point they will be able to complete the job that they started.

Out-of-Towner

When guys travel, they tend to gather numbers of the different women they meet. For some guys, they like to have women in their phones they can call whenever they visit their town. These women are called the out-of-towners because they are the women guys will call whenever they visit their towns.

I'm Not Ready Yet

Some guys are interested in a woman, but they are not ready to commit, so they keep her around until they are ready. This woman can be viewed as the "main chick" or the woman he takes most seriously. The problem is that this woman gets the most attention out of everyone in the little black book, but she has no sense of security because he will not make a commitment to her.

Nine times out of ten, this would be the woman who has been through up and downs with him and would literally stick with him no matter what. In terms of chances to be the "one," this woman has an advantage on the others, but the sad reality is that she is not guaranteed to be the one he settles down with.

The Cougar

If there is one woman that boosts the ego of a man, it would be the cougar. A cougar is an older woman who dates younger men. For some reason, a lot of guys get a kick out of having access to older women, and, for some, this is a fantasy they try to fulfill. This is because in society, it is usually socially acceptable for older men to date younger women, but it is somewhat taboo for older women to date younger men.

Guys naturally assume that older women would never give them a chance, so when they find one who gives them attention, they jump on this opportunity to fulfill their fantasy.

The Exotic Fruit

Dating across racial lines can be seen as a challenge because, over the years, a lot of people have been taught to date "their kind." For these reasons, guys find it intriguing when they are able to have access to women of other cultures. There is a general assumption that a woman of a different race would not want to be with a guy, so when he has the opportunity to land this type of woman, he typically does not hesitate.

Are You in the Little Black Book?

After reading the descriptions of the various women in the little black book, you can see that all of the women in the book are not viewed as being hoes, and they are not necessarily in negative positions. Unfortunately, a few of these women are only pursued to fulfill fantasies and not necessarily because guys really want to build a healthy relationship with them.

Since you have had an opportunity to read about the various women who are put in the little black book, the question is do you see yourself in any of these descriptions? Or have you ever been in any of these roles? Are you the out-of-towner for someone who only speaks to you when they visit your city, or are you the back-up plan who only receives a phone call whenever a guy wants to have sex with you?

I am the first to admit that the concept of the little black book is really disturbing and horrible, but the reality is that it exists for a lot of guys. While dating, you have to assure that you do not become one of the women in the little black book. This is accomplished through many of the strategies discussed throughout this book, especially:

1. Taking your time while dating and not rushing
2. Building your self-esteem so that you do not settle for less than you deserve
3. Not giving in to the pressures of having sex quickly
4. Not giving yourself to a guy before he has proven that he has your best interest at heart and that he is

serious about connecting with you emotionally, mentally, and spiritually

5. Setting standards and sticking to them

The reality is that a lot of women end up in the little black book obliviously. The truth is that, in many instances, women do what they feel is right at the moment but do not realize that they are making a mistake until it is too late. This is because some guys take advantage of them by misleading them into believing that the situation is a lot different than its true reality. Some guys make women feel that they are headed towards a relationship, but after they cross certain lines (sexually, mentally, and emotionally), they change up and head in a different direction.

Be the Little Black Book

Let me be as straightforward as I can be: I want you to understand that you deserve to be the only woman he feels the need to keep in his little black book. This does not mean that you should make a guy clear his phone of all phone numbers, but make sure that you do not settle for being one of the women in the little black book. All of a guy's attention, emotions, energy, love, affection, intimacy, and desires should be geared towards you, so if you are not receiving this, then I highly advise you to remove yourself from the situation and find someone who will make you their entire little black book.

The motto is simple: "you deserve the best and should never settle for less." So, if you are one of the women in the book, do not settle for being that. You are more than a sexual object and you are more than being a fulfilled fantasy. When a guy fully values a woman, he has no reason to keep a little black book, and the woman he is with becomes his little black book because she fulfills every desire he has.

BONUS CHAPTER

MANFAX REPORT

In my first book, *Through the Eyes of a Man: The Truth about College Dating Revealed*, I found that many of my readers thoroughly enjoyed the chapter I am about to present to you. As I was writing this book, I did not know where to place this chapter, so I decided to make it a bonus chapter for you. I hope that it blesses you and assists you on your journey of dating and finding healthy love.

If you are reading this book, I can assume that you have realized that finding a good man is not necessarily an easy process. When you step out onto the dating scene, you are bombarded with various categories of men: men in relationships, gay men, immature men, men who are known to be "no good," and unattractive men. This situation leaves only a few dateable guys from which to choose.

The small number of dateable guys creates major issues for women, because there tends to be a larger number of women trying to choose from this small pool of men. On the other hand, this creates the perfect scenario for guys, because they have a large pool of women from which to choose. In the following section, I will try to explain how guys think about women they will possibly date. This is based on my personal experiences dating and from talking to a large number of men about how they select the women they will pursue for a relationship. Hopefully, this chapter will shed light on how guys end up with certain women.

This chapter is not written to say that you need to change your life or the ways in which you do things for the purpose of landing a guy. It is my belief that a guy should love you for who you are and that you should not have to be who he wants you to be in order to be with him. What I hope you gain from this chapter is the knowledge that guys are very particular when they are in search of a woman and they do not waver a lot on their standards. My hope is that you will take the same amount of intentionality and lack of wavering when you are evaluating guys to determine if you want to be with them.

To start off, let's do a side-by-side comparison of a car lot and a woman lot to illustrate how men select their women.

Car Lot	Woman Lot
When customers walk onto a car lot, they see a large selection of cars.	When guys walk out in to the world, they see a large selection of women.

The first thing people think about is the year, make, and model of the car they desire to own.	The first thing guys notice on women is their exterior: particularly the way they dress, the way they take care of themselves cosmetically, and their cleanliness.
Customers ask for a Carfax report to check the vehicle's history, particularly checking for the following: · previous owners · mileage · accident history · reliability · other potential issues	Guys ask for the Womanfax report to check her history, particularly checking for the following: · previous relationships (who she dated in the past) · mileage (how many people she has already slept with) · accident history (determining whether she has been wounded by past bad relationships) · reliability (determining if she will remain faithful and true to her man) · other potential issues (psychoses, drama, STDs, etc.)
Customers have their credit checked to see what type of car they are capable of buying. If your credit is low, you can only afford a car with lower value, but if your credit is high, you can afford a car with high value.	Guys ask friends and associates whether they think they have what it takes to get a particular woman. This is the guy's way of doing a "credit check." If the guy has a lot going for himself, such as being smart, popular, successful, or attractive, he realizes he has access to high-quality women. If he does not possess the qualities mentioned above or other notable characteristics, he realizes he cannot have access to certain women because his "credit" is low.
Customers often test-drive cars to get a feel for how it drives, how it rides, if it handles curves well, and other things. This helps them determine whether they want to purchase the car.	Guys "talk to" and/or date women to see if they are possibly worth pursuing.

Customers consult with family and friends to validate whether they should purchase a car or to see whether their family and friends like the car.	Guys talk to friends and sometimes family about whether they should pursue a relationship or to see if family and friends like the woman they are thinking about pursuing.
Once purchased, customers are excited to showcase their vehicle if it lives up to their expectations. If it turns out to be a lemon (a car that looks good but does not function properly), they may try to return it. However, if kept as a lemon, they usually will not take good care of it or put effort into rebuilding it.	Once dating or in a formal relationship, guys are excited to showcase their woman to others if they live up to their expectations. If they do not meet their expectations, they may try to end the relationship. However, if they stay in a relationship and the woman does not meet their expectations, they might possibly treat the woman badly.

The WomanFax Report

The WomanFax report is arguably one of the most important aspects of dating for men. WomanFax reports are run daily and are tools used by guys to determine if they will date a woman. There is no secure way for a man to know if a woman is worth dating, but if he completes a thorough background check on her, he can discover many important things before making a decision about pursuing her. One of the biggest fears for men is that the woman he settles down with is an undercover whore and has slept with multiple guys.

Previous Relationships

When guys examine a woman's previous relationships, they look for a few things, including who she dated, for how long she dated these other guys, and the nature of the relationships. First, guys want to know who the woman dated, because he needs to make sure that he is not getting a woman who was rejected by other guys. Men hate to know that women have dated guys with status such as athletes, rappers, bad boys, pretty boys, and popular guys in the community. Sometimes, men perceive the women who have dated these guys as having groupie tendencies and they think they were only with these guys for their status or money. Because men have egos, they cannot date these ladies; they do not want to be seen as the guy who dates a woman whom the popular guy did not want (a hand-me-down).

Second, guys want to know for how long a woman dated her previous boyfriends. If she was in long-term relationships, guys can overlook her having sex with these guys because it was stable and there was a formal commitment. If she has been in four relationships within a year and has had sex with all of them, guys perceive this as her not making good decisions and giving too much of herself too quickly. Typically, guys do not want these women. On the other hand, if she had three boyfriends over six years (averaging two years per boyfriend), guys realize that she invested in these exes, and most men acknowledge that intimacy is a normal part of the progression of a two-year relationship.

Finally, guys want to know the nature of the relationship. If a woman was a "real girlfriend" in an openly committed relationship, guys can respect this. Contrarily, if she was in a situation where she did not have a title but functioned as a girlfriend and gave a lot of herself to him, this can bother men. A man's ego will make him ask the question, "Why do we have to settle down with a woman and make her our girlfriend, when the last guy got everything out of her without making her his girlfriend?" Please note that most of the things that bother guys and cause them to dismiss women are triggered by their egos. Although this may not be fair to women and is shallow of men, it is a reality of how guys select women.

Mileage

For the purpose of this guide, mileage is defined as the number of guys with whom a woman has had sex. Ideally, most guys would prefer to settle down with a woman who had no sexual partners. Although guys know there are virgins in the world, they realize this expectation is unrealistic. Since a lot of people have already had sex, most men try to find women who have slept with a minimal number of men.

I have participated in several panel discussions regarding dating, and the question about mileage always emerges. I always state that there is no set number of sexual partners a woman is allowed to have in the eyes of men. Each guy has a personal threshold about the mileage he will allow, but I will say that after a woman's count leaves one hand (five guys), it can become disturbing for men.

I have noticed that age plays a major factor in the number of guys acceptable for a woman to sleep with. The older she is, the more lenient guys tend to be with the number of men she has slept with. I am almost sure that an 18-year-old woman having slept with more than eight guys would be disturbing to most men.

Accident History

Guys look for women's accident histories to determine if they have been damaged. The truth is that some guys think damaged women are hard to deal with and require a lot of work. Some guys are not willing to put in the work it would take to help repair a damaged woman and would rather seek women who are not damaged. There are some issues that damaged women bring to a relationship that can be a turn-off to guys. For example, women who have trust issues and overreact to minor situations as a result of bad previous relationships can be disturbing to many guys. Guys' big egos make them ask the question, "Why do we have to expend our energy and rebuild a woman, when another guy caused the damage?"

Reliability

Guys check the reliability of women because they do not want to open themselves up to women who have not been faithful in the past. If a woman has cheated on a previous boyfriend, guys assume that she will cheat on them. If a woman broke up with her previous boyfriend for no valid reason, guys tend to assume that she will break up with them for no valid reason. Although men may not admit it, many of them have fragile hearts and will take every precaution to make sure they do not get broken. This can be seen as a major contradiction to the way guys sometime treat women's hearts.

Other

Guys also check for other things during their WomanFax investigation. For instance, most guys try to determine if a woman is psychotic or filled with drama. If a woman has slashed her ex-boyfriend's tires or fought other women for a guy, most guys assume that she will treat their relationship the same way.

My Advice

I know a lot of the material in this chapter may seem like a major contradiction on behalf of men. For example, guys want women with low mileage, but have high mileage themselves. However, I encourage you to treat guys the same way they treat you. It is my belief that women should do a ManFax report on the men they are thinking about dating. Do a complete background check on guys to learn as much as you can before making a decision to invest in him mentally, emotionally, and sexually. I think a lot of women make decisions too quickly, without knowing much about the guys they are dealing with. It is my belief that if you do a proper ManFax report and make a decision based on the results, it will lower your chances of getting with a guy who will hurt you. I have noticed that a lot of women have yellow and red flags in their face but disregard or ignore them and choose to pursue the relationship. By not doing a ManFax report or disregarding the results, you increase your chances of being hurt and/or damaged. Be sure to take your time and get to know a man before you invest in him; I promise it will benefit you in the long run.

FAQs
FREQUENTLY ASKED QUESTIONS

- **Why do men cheat?**

I am often asked, "Why do men continuously cheat?" I always say, I can list off a ton of reasons why men cheat, but there is one that sticks out in my head that a lot of men have expressed to me: **because they can**. I know this response is probably a straight slap in the face, because a situation that is so complex for a lot of women seems to be very simple for men.

A lot of guys cheat because they know they can without any major ramifications for it. Sure, a woman may get upset, she may bust out his windows, she may call the other women (while the other woman will probably already know about her), or she may even stop talking to him for a bit. The reality is that after the smoke clears, most guys know that the relationship will be back on track in a few weeks (maybe with a few trust issues, but it will still be together).

I am one to believe in forgiveness and, in some situation, second chances, but if you find yourself on chance number three or four, then you are helping to perpetuate this notion that men can get away with cheating. The reality is that there have to be fruitful consequences to actions and not weightless threats that guys can see through and can tell are bluffs. I can assure you that the results from a "zero tolerance" policy will be a lot better than recurring forgiveness.

Let's further discuss cheating.

Some men will tell you that they made a mistake when they cheated. When I think of someone making a mistake, I think of things such as misspelling a word, failing to remember someone's birthday, or forgetting to feed a pet before going to work. These are errors that are not intentional but may create some type of misunderstanding. Over the years, I have noticed that many people have added "cheating in a committed relationship" to the list of mistakes that people make.

I have given relationship advice to several women who have experienced the pain of a cheating man. Their man's typical response for cheating was, "I made a mistake." This leads me to ask the question, "How can a person make a mistake if they knew what they were doing?"

Cheating is not a mistake, it is a bad choice. A person does not mistakenly take their clothes off, nor do they mistakenly engage in intercourse. These things are called choices. Allowing cheating to be viewed as a mistake sometime takes away some of the severity from the offense, because it makes it look less intentional. A lot of cheaters do not use the word "choice," because the word "choice" makes their actions more intentional, resulting in their mates being less lenient.

To put this into perspective, think about this. If a person pointed a gun at someone and intentionally pulled the trigger, that person cannot call it a mistake; instead, it is viewed as a bad choice. Conversely, if a person dropped a loaded gun on the floor and it fired and hit someone, it could be viewed as a mistake. Although both people caused a gun to fire and shoot someone, the courts would respond to these cases differently because of the intentions behind the firing.

Cheating is an intentional action, and people should be held accountable for their actions. I am not saying that a relationship cannot be repaired after infidelity, but allowing someone to downplay their actions by calling it a mistake is not acceptable.

- **Why do guys choose wild girls over respectable women?**

I can admit that there are some men who pursue women who are wild and show them lot of attention. The truth is that, although they get a lot of attention, they generally do not get affection. Attention is a surface-level acknowledgment, and some guys acknowledge these women for the purposes of fulfilling their desires and fantasies. On the other hand, most men will never settle down permanently with these wild girls. What is usually lacking from a situation where a guy is dating a wild woman is affection. There tends to be a lack of connection, love, growth, and sincerity in these relationships.

On the other hand, respectable women may not receive as much attention, but it is not for the reasons one may think. A lot of people think that guys are not interested in respectable women, because they do not show them as much attention. This is not necessarily the case. The truth is that guys know they have to come correct when approaching respectable women, and sometimes they do not want to put in the work. These guys would rather settle for a wild girl temporarily until he feels he is prepared for a respectable woman. Most guys will never marry the wild girl; instead, they will pursue a respectable woman when they are ready to settle down and get married.

One question I always pose is, *when you see these men with wild girls, are their relationships really healthy?* In my experience, these relationships have a lot of trust issues, there is no security in them, and they seem somewhat lifeless. If you are battling with being single and not receiving a lot of attention, I encourage you to stay strong and stick to your values. No man is worth you lowering yourself and your value for because he does not have the maturity or courage to pursue you. Remember that you are a queen, and queens do not let just anyone have access to them. There are good men out there who are only looking for respectable women, but it may take time and a proper evaluation (which I hoped you learned in this book).

- **Why did the book not cover "courting," and isn't it the same as dating?**

In my opinion, dating and courting are two different things and serve two different purposes. It is my belief that dating leads up to courting, hence the reason it was not discussed in this book. Dating is more casual in nature and it is to get you to the point of becoming an official couple. Once you become an official couple, this is when an actual courtship begins. Courting is defined as the period in a couple's relationship which precedes their engagement and marriage, or establishment of an agreed-upon relationship of a more enduring kind (Wikipedia). Based on this definition, you can see that courtship has an emphasis on engagement and marriage. So dating leads to official relationships, and courting leads to engagement and marriage.

- **Why does this book not address building a healthy relationship?**

I did not include any advice about building a relationship after it becomes official because I believe this conversation should be for both individuals and not only one. A healthy relationship cannot be built if only one person is working to improve themself. A book is in the works for building healthy relationships (official relationships), and it will be for couples to read and not individuals.

- **What does it take to land a good man?**

Landing a good man is not about you doing things for a guy for the purpose of making him want you; it is about doing things for yourself so he would want you. Good guys want women who build themselves and not women who alter themselves to try to please a man.

MORE BONUSES
A FEW MORE GOODIES

7 Steps Toward Gaining Respect

Realize Your Value. – If you do not set a value for yourself, others will set that value for you.

Expect Nothing but the Best from Others.

Set High Standards for Yourself and Others.

Present Yourself in a Suitable Way at All Times.

Easy is not an option. Anything that is to be respected should come with hard work.

Choose Wisely Who You Associate Yourself With.

Treat Others with Respect.

The ABCs of a Healthy Relationship

A – Affection
B – Balance
C – Communication
D – Date Nights
E – Emotional Support
F – Flirting (with each other)
G – God
H – Honesty
I – Intimacy
J – Jokes
K – Kisses
L – Love/Laughter
M – Mental Stimulation

N – Nice to Each Other
O – Openness
P – Prayer
Q – Quality Time
R – Respect
S – Security
T – Trust
U – Understanding
V – Vision
W – Wisdom
X – XOXO (Hugs and Kisses)
Y – Youthfulness
Z – Zeal

ABOUT THE AUTHOR

DR. COREY GUYTON

Dr. Corey Guyton is an author, speaker, educator, husband, father, and the founder of www.thegenuinescholar.com. He has spoken at colleges, universities, and conferences throughout the country about healthy dating/relationships, self-respect, and self-worth. He is also the founder of and facilitator for the *Reset My Heart* Relationship Seminars (www.resetmyheart.com). In his free time, he writes for various websites and blogs and he is also the author of *Through the Eyes of a Man: The Truth about College Dating Revealed to Women*.

Dr. Guyton graduated from Clayton State University in 2005 with a Bachelor of Applied Science in Technology Management. He immediately enrolled in the Master of Education program in College Student Personnel at the University of Louisville, from which he graduated in 2007. Despite others telling him he was too young to enter a Ph.D program, he stepped out on faith and applied to the Higher Education Leadership doctorate program at Indiana State University. In only three and a half years, Dr. Guyton completed his Ph.D from Indiana State University in 2011, making him the youngest person to ever complete the program.

In June of 2011, Dr. Guyton married the love of his life, Dr. Chutney Guyton. They had their first child in September of 2013, a beautiful son named Camden. They also have a cat named Mary Jane Guyton. Dr. Guyton offers keynote speeches, workshops, and training sessions for individuals or groups. For more information, visit www.thegenuinescholar.com and like his page on Facebook www.facebook.com/iwontsettle.